OUTDOOR GAS GRIDDLE
Cookbook

OUTDOOR GAS GRIDDLE

Cookbook

Tasty & Affordable **Outdoor Gas Griddle** Recipes to Become Your Favorite Family's Chef

PHIL JACKSON

© Copyright 2023 by **Phil Jackson** - All rights reserved.

———————————————

This document is geared towards providing exact and reliable information in regard to the topic and issue covered. The publication is sold with the idea that the publisher is not required to render accounting, officially permitted, or otherwise, qualified services. If advice is necessary, legal or professional, a practiced individual in the profession should be ordered.

From a Declaration of Principles which was accepted and approved equally by a Committee of the American Bar Association and a Committee of Publishers and Associations. In no way is it legal to reproduce, duplicate, or transmit any part of this document in either electronic means or in printed format. Recording of this publication is strictly prohibited, and any storage of this document is not allowed unless with written permission from the publisher. All rights reserved.

The information provided herein is stated to be truthful and consistent, in that any liability, in terms of inattention or otherwise, by any usage or abuse of any policies, processes, or directions contained within is the solitary and utter responsibility of the recipient reader. Under no circumstances will any legal responsibility or blame be held against the publisher for any reparation, damages, or monetary loss due to the information herein, either directly or indirectly.

Respective authors own all copyrights not held by the publisher. The information herein is offered for informational purposes solely and is universal as such. The presentation of the information is without a contract or any type of guaranteed assurance. The trademarks that are used are without any consent, and the publication of the trademark is without permission or backing by the trademark owner. All trademarks and brands within this book are for clarifying purposes only and are owned by the owners themselves, not affiliated with this document

Contents

Introduction 9

CHAPTER ONE
Breakfast Recipes 18

CHAPTER TWO
Burger's Recipes 25

CHAPTER THREE
Vegetables & Side dishes 32

CHAPTER FOUR
Beef Recipes 39

CHAPTER FIVE
Pork Recipes 46

CHAPTER SIX
Chicken Recipes 53

CHAPTER SEVEN
Poultry Recipes 60

CHAPTER EIGHT
Lamb Recipes 64

CHAPTER NINE
Wild Game Recipes 68

CHAPTER TEN
Seafood Recipes 75

CHAPTER ELEVEN
Dessert Recipes 82

Conclusion 89

Index 90

THE AUTHOR

Phil Jackson is a passionate outdoor chef from Texas. As a father, he loves nothing more than sharing his delicious recipes with his family and friends, and his love for grilling and BBQ has led him to participate in some of the best BBQ festivals in the country, where he honed his skills and picked up new techniques from some of the top pitmasters in the business. With over a decade of grilling experience, Phil has become a master of the art of griddling, and he is excited to share his knowledge and expertise with his readers.

In this comprehensive guide, Phil will teach you everything you need to know to master the gas griddle, from basic techniques to advanced recipes. You'll learn how to use and maintain your griddle, select the right ingredients, prepare them for grilling, how to treat your meats, and how to achieve the perfect temperature and timing. There is also a variety of recipes ranging from seafood, white and dark meats, wild game, multi-cuisines, breakfasts, side dishes, vegetarian food, vegan dishes, and even desserts. With Phil's help, you'll be able to create delicious and affordable meals that will be enjoyed by your family and friends. Whether you're a beginner or a seasoned griller, this cookbook is sure to become your go-to guide for all your grilling needs.

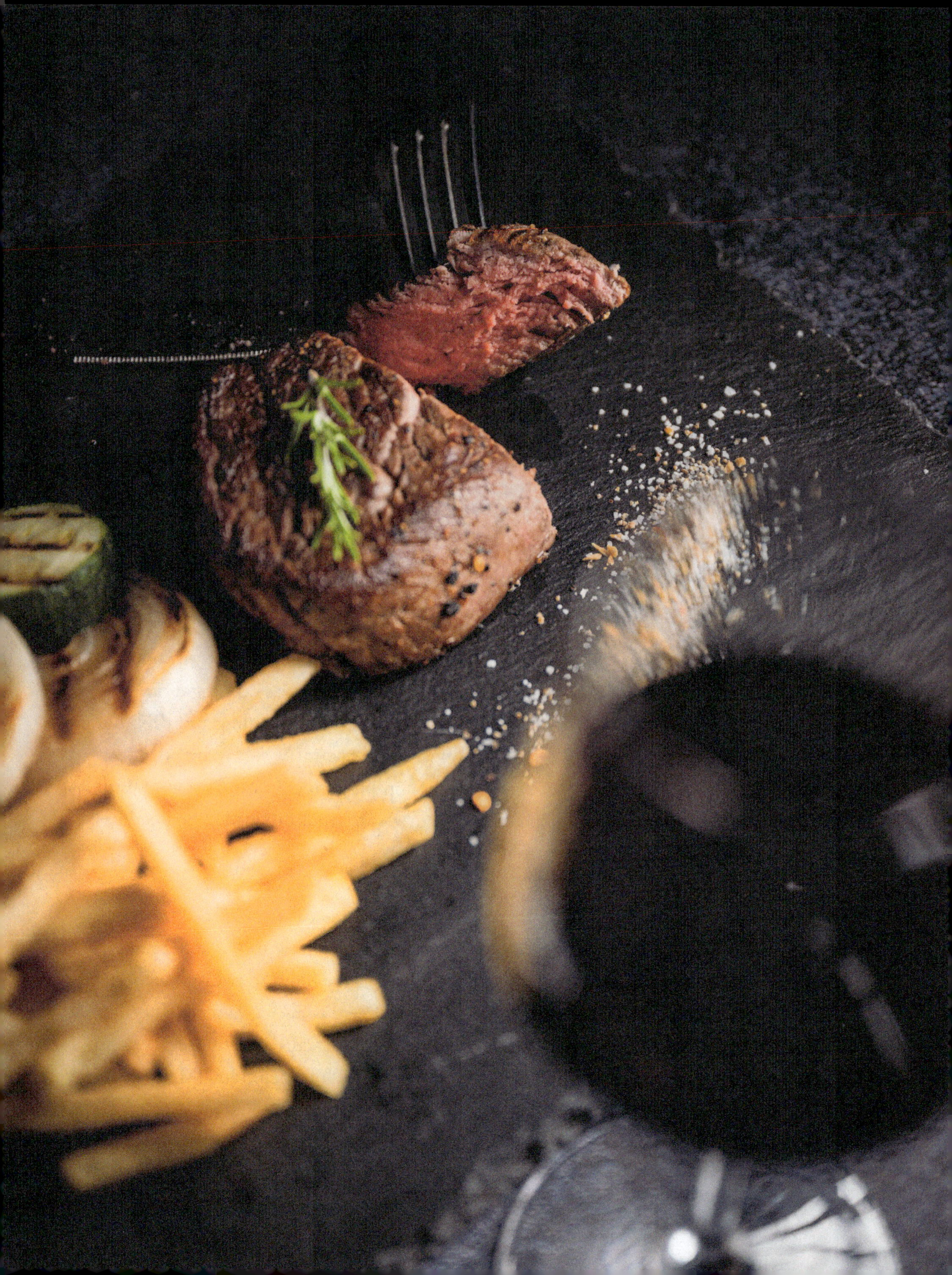

Introduction

There is something undeniably satisfying about standing in front of a griddle, spatula in hand, as the aroma of sizzling burgers and steaks fills the air. The heat, the sizzling meat, and the smell of gas and char providing a delicious meal for the hungry bellies around is an incredibly satisfying feeling. As the person in charge of the grill or griddle, you have the ability to make a lasting impression on those around you; you have direct access to their taste buds and stomachs, and consequentially their minds, so you better take your role seriously and ensure you know what you're doing.

A gas griddle is a flat cooking surface that is powered by natural gas or propane. It is typically used for grilling and searing a variety of foods, such as burgers, steaks, chicken, and vegetables, and is often used in outdoor cooking: backyard patios, picnics, and tailgate parties. They are a convenient and easy way to cook large quantities of a wide range of dishes and are often preferred by professional chefs and home cooks alike due to their even heat distribution and speed.

GAS GRIDDLE VS WOODEN PELLET GRILL

One major difference between the gas griddle and the wooden pellet grill is the fuel source. A gas griddle is powered by natural gas or propane, while a wood pellet grill uses wood pellets as fuel and this affects the result of the dishes. For instance, there is a big difference in temperature and heat distribution. Gas griddles generally heat up more quickly and provide more even heat distribution, making it easier to cook foods evenly and to the desired doneness. Wood pellet grills on the other hand require more time to heat up and may have hotter and cooler spots, which can make it more difficult to achieve consistent results.

In terms of maintenance and upkeep, gas griddles are generally easier to maintain than wood pellet grills, because of the ash that the wood pellets produce on burning. Hence, the wood pellet grills may require frequent cleaning, and the pellets need to be refilled.

In terms of taste, the wood chips produce a smoky flavor, that elevates the quality of many dishes, but it doesn't suit all recipes. And some people just don't like the smokiness, so the quality of the outcome is subjective. But, with wood pellet grills, you are not going to escape the grill's flavor on your food.

GAS GRIDDLE VS CHARCOAL GRILL

The charcoal grill, just like the wooden pellets, gives out a distinct flavor that may or may not suit the dish and to an extent is an acquired taste. The charcoal grills are easier to transport and use at picnics, but the process of getting the charcoal briquettes lit and evenly distributing the cinders is an art that only experience can teach you. And because you rely on coal for heat, it is a challenge to control the temperature and heat distribution.

Operating and using these grills can be more time-consuming and require more maintenance than gas griddles. They typically take longer to heat up and may have hotter and cooler spots, which can make it more difficult to achieve consistent cooking results. They also produce ash, which requires regular cleaning and maintenance.

THE BENEFITS OF COOKING ON A GRIDDLE

We've already touched upon many of the advantages gas griddles have over grills, but if you are yet to get yourself one, here is a list of reasons why you've got to. The described features are also crucial factors that you have to take into consideration before you buy yourself a grill, doesn't matter if it's gas or charcoal.

1. Quick and even heat: Gas griddles heat up quickly and provide even heat distribution, making it easier to cook foods evenly and to the desired doneness.
2. Versatility: Gas griddles can be used to cook a wide range of foods, from pancakes and eggs to burgers and steaks.
3. Convenience: Gas griddles are easy to use and require minimal maintenance. They also have large cooking surfaces, allowing you to cook multiple items at once.
4. Energy efficiency: Gas griddles are more energy efficient than charcoal grills, as they do not require the use of lighter fluid and produce less ash.
5. Safety: Gas griddles are generally safer to use than charcoal grills, as there is no risk of coal or ash falling out and causing a fire hazard.
6. Portable: Gas griddles can be easily transported and used at picnics, tailgate parties, and other outdoor events.
7. Customization: Some gas griddles come with additional features, such as side burners or warming racks, allowing for more customization and versatility in cooking.

THE FUNDAMENTALS OF OUTDOOR GAS GRIDDLES

Whether you're a seasoned griddle chef or new to the world of outdoor cooking, this section is for you. Gas griddles are a convenient and easy way to cook a wide range of dishes, and understanding the basics is essential for getting the most out of your griddle. Here, we will cover the key features and considerations when using an outdoor gas griddle, as well as some tips and tricks for successful griddle cooking. So grab your spatula and let's get started!

THE BASICS

Here are some essentials on getting a gas griddle ready for use, that you've got to know:

1. **Assemble your griddle:** If you are using a new or recently purchased gas griddle, make sure to follow the manufacturer's instructions for assembly. This may involve attaching the legs, attaching any additional features (such as side burners), and attaching the gas hose and regulator.

2. **Check for gas leaks:** Before using your gas griddle for the first time, it is important to check for gas leaks. To do this, apply a solution of soap and water to the connections on the gas hose and regulator. If you see any bubbles forming, there is a gas leak present and you will need to fix it before using the griddle.

3. **Preheat the griddle:** Most gas griddles have a preheat setting, which allows you to heat the griddle surface to the desired temperature before cooking. Preheating the griddle ensures that it is hot enough to properly cook and sear your food.

④ **Season the griddle:** Before cooking on a new or recently cleaned griddle, it is a good idea to "season" the surface. This involves applying a thin layer of oil to the griddle surface and heating it up. This helps to prevent food from sticking and also helps to create a non-stick surface over time.

⑤ **Set the heat:** Gas griddles typically have adjustable heat settings, allowing you to control the temperature of the cooking surface. It is important to set the heat correctly for the type of food you are cooking, as different foods require different cooking temperatures.

⑥ **Clean and maintain the griddle:** After each use, it is important to clean and maintain your gas griddle to keep it in good working condition. This may involve wiping down the surface, checking the gas connections for leaks, and replacing any worn or damaged parts.

QUICK START AND TIPS

Now that we know our basics, it's time to graduate and become masters. Here are a few tips that have been picked up through years of experience that is going to help you look like the master you're about to become.

① Place the griddle on a flat, stable surface: It is important to make sure that your gas griddle is placed on a flat, stable surface to ensure that it does not tip over or move during use.

② Check the fuel level: Make sure that you have enough gas or propane to cook your desired amount of food.

③ As mentioned in the previous section, preheating the griddle is important to ensure that it is hot enough to properly cook and sear your food, if you are using a new or recently cleaned griddle season it before cooking to prevent food from sticking and to create a non-stick surface over time, and adjust the heat settings to the appropriate level for the type of food you are cooking.

④ Use a griddle spatula that has a flat surface and beveled edges, and is ideal for flipping and moving food on a griddle.

⑤ Keep the griddle clean. Wipe down the griddle surface after each use to remove any excess food or grease. This will help to prevent flare-ups and ensure that your griddle stays in good working condition.

⑥ And don't forget to have fun and get creative. Don't be afraid to experiment with different recipes and techniques to find what works best for you.

GAS GRIDDLE COOKING TABLE

Now that we're all set for the cooking, here is a quick table showing the temperature and time required to cook certain foods. Please note that these are just the general guidelines and actual cooking times may vary depending on the size and thickness of the meat, the recipe, and the desired level of doneness. I would also recommend you use a meat thermometer to ensure that the meat has reached the desired internal temperature.

MEAT TYPE	RECOMMENDED COOKING TEMPERATURE	RECOMMENDED COOKING TIME
Burgers (beef, turkey, veggie)	375-400°F	4-6 minutes per side
Steaks (beef, pork, lamb)	400-450°F	4-6 minutes per side
Pork chops	400-450°F	6-8 minutes per side
Chicken	375-400°F	6-8 minutes per side
Turkey	375-400°F	6-8 minutes per side
Duck	400-450°F	4-6 minutes per side
Rabbit	375-400°F	6-8 minutes per side
Shrimp	375-400°F	2-3 minutes per side
Salmaon	375-400°F	4-6 minutes per side
Vegetables (zucchini, bell peppers, onions)	375-400°F	4-6 minutes per side
Pulled pork	275-300°F	6-8 hours
Slow cooked dark meat	275-300°F	6-8 hours
Elk	400-450°F	4-6 minutes per side
Boar	400-450°F	4-6 minutes per side

MAINTENANCE

Proper maintenance is essential to ensure that your gas griddle stays in good working condition and continues to perform at its best. Here are some tips for maintaining your gas griddle:

1. Clean the griddle surface after each use: Wipe down the griddle surface with a damp cloth or sponge to remove any excess food or grease. This will help to prevent flare-ups and ensure that your griddle stays in good condition.

2. Use a griddle scraper: A griddle scraper is a tool specifically designed to remove stuck-on food and debris from the griddle surface. It is an effective and safe way to keep your griddle clean without damaging the surface.

3. Remove excess grease: After each use, it is important to remove excess grease from the griddle surface and grease tray. This can be done using a griddle scraper, a sponge, or a paper towel.

4. Store your griddle properly: When not in use, make sure to cover your gas griddle with a protective cover to keep it clean and protected from the elements.

5. Check for gas leaks: Regularly check the gas hose and regulator for any signs of wear or damage. If you notice any leaks, make sure to fix them immediately.

6. Replace worn or damaged parts: If any parts of your gas griddle are worn or damaged, make sure to replace them as soon as possible to ensure that your griddle stays in good working condition.

By following these maintenance tips, you can help to extend the life of your gas griddle and ensure that it continues to perform at its best.

CONVERSION TABLES

We are almost done with this section and before we get on to the recipes, here are a few tables with the conversion of various units of measurements that may come in handy:

TEMPERATURE CONVERSIONS

FAHRENHEIT	CELSIUS
250°F	121.1°C
275°F	135.0°C
300°F	148.9°C
325°F	162.8°C
350°F	176.7°C
375°F	190.6°C
400°F	204.4°C
425°F	218.3°C
450°F	232.2°C

WEIGHT CONVERSIONS

POUNDS	KILOGRAMS
1 lb	0.45 kg
2 lb	0.91 kg
3 lb	1.36 kg
4 lb	1.81 kg
5 lb	2.27 kg

VOLUME CONVERSIONS

FLUID OUNCES	MILLILITERS
1 fl oz	29.57 ml
2 fl oz	59.15 ml
3 fl oz	88.72 ml
4 fl oz	118.29 ml
5 fl oz	147.87 ml

Chapter 01

BREAKFAST RECIPES

PERFECT SCRAMBLED EGGS

Scrambled eggs are a classic breakfast dish that can be easily prepared on a gas griddle. They are a quick and easy meal that can be enjoyed any time of day.

SERVING
1-2 people

PREPARATION
10 min

GRIDDLING TIME
5-7 min

GRIDDLING TEMP
375-400°F

Ingredients

2-3 large eggs
1 tablespoon butter or oil
Salt and pepper, to taste

Directions

1. Crack the eggs into a small bowl and beat them lightly with a fork.
2. Place the butter or oil on the griddle and allow it to melt.
3. Pour the beaten eggs onto the griddle and use a spatula to scrape the bottom of the griddle as the eggs cook.
4. Once the eggs start to set, use the spatula to gently fold them over and scramble them until they are fully cooked.
5. Season the eggs with salt and pepper, to taste.
6. Serve the scrambled eggs hot, with your choice of accompaniments such as toast, bacon, or fruit.

Nutritional Value (Per Serving)

Calories: 150
Protein: 12 g
Fat: 11 g
Carbs: 1 g
Fiber: 0 g
Sugars: 1 g

BUTTERMILK PANCAKES

Soft and fluffy on the inside, with a golden brown crust on the outside, these pancakes are sure to satisfy your cravings.

SERVING
10 medium-sized pancakes

PREPARATION
15 min

GRIDDLING TIME
10-15 min

GRIDDLING TEMP
375-400°F

Ingredients

1 cup all-purpose flour
1 teaspoon baking powder
1/2 teaspoon baking soda
1/2 teaspoon salt
1 cup buttermilk
1 large egg
2 tablespoons butter, melted
1 teaspoon vanilla extract
Cooking spray or butter, for greasing the griddle

Nutritional Value (Per Serving)

Calories: 150
Protein: 4 g
Fat: 6 g
Carbs: 22 g
Fiber: 1 g

Directions

1. In a medium mixing bowl, whisk together the flour, baking powder, baking soda, and salt.
2. In a separate mixing bowl, whisk together the buttermilk, egg, melted butter, and vanilla extract.
3. Add the wet ingredients to the dry ingredients and stir until just combined. The batter should be slightly lumpy.
4. Heat the griddle over medium heat and lightly grease it with cooking spray or butter.
5. Pour the batter onto the griddle in 1/4 cup increments, using a spoon or ladle to spread it into circles.
6. Cook the pancakes for 2-3 minutes, or until bubbles start to form on the surface.
7. Flip the pancakes and cook for an additional 1-2 minutes, or until golden brown on the second side.
8. Remove the pancakes from the griddle and place them on a plate. Repeat the process with the remaining batter, lightly greasing the griddle as needed.
9. Serve the pancakes hot, with your choice of toppings such as syrup, butter, fruit, or whipped cream.

STRAWBERRY, BANANA, AND HAZELNUT-CHOCOLATE CREPES

This classic French dish is filled with fresh strawberries, bananas, and a rich and creamy hazelnut-chocolate spread and makes a great breakfast.

SERVING
8 crepes

PREPARATION
20 min

GRIDDLING TIME
10–15 min

GRIDDLING TEMP
375–400°F

Ingredients

1 cup all-purpose flour
1 cup milk
1 large egg
2 tablespoons sugar
1 teaspoon vanilla extract
1/4 teaspoon salt
1 cup fresh strawberries, sliced
1 medium banana, sliced
1/2 cup hazelnut-chocolate spread
Cooking spray or butter, for greasing the griddle

Nutritional Value (Per Serving)

Calories: 250
Protein: 6 g
Fat: 9 g
Carbs: 41 g
Fiber: 2 g
Sugars: 21 g

Directions

1. In a medium mixing bowl, whisk together the flour, milk, egg, sugar, vanilla extract, and salt.
2. Heat the griddle over medium heat and lightly grease it with cooking spray or butter.
3. Pour about 1/4 cup of the crepe batter onto the griddle, using a spoon or ladle to spread it into a thin, even circle.
4. Cook the crepe for 1-2 minutes, or until the edges start to turn golden brown.
5. Flip the crepe and cook for an additional 30 seconds, or until cooked through.
6. Remove the crepe from the griddle and place it on a plate. Repeat the process with the remaining batter, lightly greasing the griddle as needed.
7. Once all the crepes are cooked, fill each crepe with a few slices of strawberry, banana, and a spoonful of hazelnut-chocolate spread.
8. Roll the crepes up and serve them hot.

STEAK AND MUSHROOM CREPES

Though crepes are mostly associated with sweets, this dish, with a savory flavor showcases another dimension that can be added to this French delecasy.

SERVING
8 crepes

PREPARATION
30 min

GRIDDLING TIME
10-15 min

GRIDDLING TEMP
375-400°F

Ingredients

1 cup all-purpose flour
1 cup milk
1 large egg
1/4 teaspoon salt
1/2 pound thin-sliced steak, cut into strips
1 cup mushrooms, sliced
1 tablespoon butter or oil
1/4 cup shredded cheese (optional)
Cooking spray or butter, for greasing the griddle

Nutritional Value (Per Serving)

Calories: 250
Protein: 20 g
Fat: 9 g
Carbs: 21 g
Fiber: 2 g
Sugars: 4 g

Directions

1. In a medium mixing bowl, whisk together the flour, milk, egg, and salt.
2. Heat the griddle over medium heat and lightly grease it with cooking spray or butter.
3. Pour about 1/4 cup of the crepe batter onto the griddle, using a spoon or ladle to spread it into a thin, even circle.
4. Cook the crepe for 1-2 minutes, or until the edges start to turn golden brown.
5. Flip the crepe and cook for an additional 30 seconds, or until cooked through.
6. Remove the crepe from the griddle and place it on a plate. Repeat the process with the remaining batter, lightly greasing the griddle as needed.
7. While the crepes are cooking, heat the butter or oil in a pan over medium heat. Add the steak and mushrooms and sauté until the steak is cooked to your desired level of doneness and the mushrooms are tender.
8. Once all the crepes are cooked, fill each crepe with a few slices of steak and mushrooms. Sprinkle with cheese, if using.
9. Roll the crepes up and serve them hot

GRIDDLED CHEESE BREAKFAST BURRITO

Filled with fluffy scrambled eggs, melted cheese, and a variety of toppings, this griddled cheese burrito is sure to hit the spot.

SERVING
1 burrito

PREPARATION
10 min

GRIDDLING TIME
5-10 min

GRIDDLING TEMP
375-400°F

Ingredients

1 large flour tortilla
2 large eggs
1/4 cup shredded cheese
2 tablespoons diced cooked bacon, sausage, or ham (optional)
2 tablespoons diced bell pepper, onion, or tomato (optional)
Cooking spray or butter, for greasing the griddle

Nutritional Value (Per Serving)

Calories: 350
Protein: 20 g
Fat: 20 g
Carbs: 26 g
Fiber: 2 g
Sugars: 4 g

Directions

1. Heat the griddle over medium heat and lightly grease it with cooking spray or butter.
2. In a small mixing bowl, beat the eggs until well scrambled.
3. Place the tortilla on the griddle and sprinkle the cheese over one-half of the tortilla.
4. Pour the eggs over the cheese and add the optional toppings, if using.
5. Fold the tortilla in half over the filling and press gently to seal.
6. Cook the burrito for 2-3 minutes, or until the bottom is golden brown and the cheese is melted.
7. Flip the burrito and cook for an additional 1-2 minutes, or until the second side is golden brown.
8. Remove the burrito from the griddle and cut it in half. Serve hot.

CHORIZO BREAKFAST TACOS

If you love Mexican food and breakfast, these tacos filled with spicy chorizo sausage, fluffy scrambled eggs, and a variety of toppings are sure to satisfy your love.

SERVING
4 tacos

PREPARATION
15 min

GRIDDLING TIME
5-10 min

GRIDDLING TEMP
375-400°F

Ingredients

4 small corn tortillas
1/2 cup diced chorizo sausage
2 large eggs
1/4 cup diced onion
1/4 cup diced bell pepper
1/4 cup diced tomato
1/4 cup shredded cheese
2 tablespoons chopped fresh cilantro
1 tablespoon butter or oil
Cooking spray or butter, for greasing the griddle

Nutritional Value (Per Serving)

Calories: 300
Protein: 20 g
Fat: 20 g
Carbs: 20 g
Fiber: 2 g
Sugars: 4 g

Directions

1. Heat the griddle over medium heat and lightly grease it with cooking spray or butter.
2. In a small pan, melt the butter or heat the oil over medium heat. Add the chorizo and cook until it is browned and fully cooked.
3. In a small mixing bowl, beat the eggs until well scrambled.
4. Place a tortilla on the griddle and sprinkle some cheese over half of the tortilla.
5. Pour the eggs over the cheese and top with the chorizo, onion, bell pepper, tomato, and cilantro.
6. Fold the tortilla in half over the filling and press gently to seal.
7. Cook the taco for 2-3 minutes, or until the bottom is golden brown and the cheese is melted.
8. Flip the taco and cook for an additional 1-2 minutes, or until the second side is golden brown.
9. Repeat the process with the remaining tortillas and filling ingredients.
10. Serve the tacos hot, with additional toppings as desired.

Chapter 02

BURGER RECIPES

JUICY TEXAS BURGERS

Texas-style burgers are known for their bold, hearty flavors. Made with a mixture of ground beef, spices, and diced onions, these burgers are juicy and flavorful.

SERVING
4 burgers

PREPARATION
15 min

GRIDDLING TIME
10-15 min

GRIDDLING TEMP
400-425°F

Ingredients

1 1/2 pounds ground beef
1/2 cup diced onion
1 teaspoon ground cumin
1 teaspoon chili powder
1/2 teaspoon salt
1/4 teaspoon black pepper
4 hamburger buns
4 slices cheddar cheese (optional)
Lettuce, tomato, pickles, and condiments, for serving (optional)

Nutritional Value (Per Serving)

Calories: 400
Protein: 30 g
Fat: 25 g
Carbs: 30 g
Fiber: 2 g
Sugars: 4 g

Directions

1. In a large mixing bowl, combine the ground beef, onion, cumin, chili powder, salt, and pepper. Mix well to combine.
2. Divide the mixture into 4 equal portions and shape each portion into a patty.
3. Place the patties on the griddle and cook for 5-6 minutes per side, or until they are cooked to your desired level of doneness.
4. During the last minute of cooking, add a slice of cheese to each patty if using.
5. Place the buns on the griddle, cut side down, and toast for 1-2 minutes, or until they are lightly toasted.
6. Assemble the burgers by placing a patty on the bottom bun and topping it with lettuce, tomato, pickles, and condiments, if desired.
7. Serve the burgers hot, with additional toppings as desired.

PORKY BURGER

Made with a mixture of ground pork and beef, topped with a tangy BBQ sauce and crispy bacon, this burger is packed with flavor and moisture.

SERVING
4 burgers

PREPARATION
15 min

GRIDDLING TIME
10-15 min

GRIDDLING TEMP
400-425°F

Ingredients

1 pound ground pork
1/2 pound ground beef
1/2 cup diced onion
1 teaspoon ground cumin
1 teaspoon chili powder
1/2 teaspoon salt
1/4 teaspoon black pepper
4 hamburger buns
4 slices cheddar cheese (optional)
4 slices bacon, cooked until crispy
1/2 cup BBQ sauce
Lettuce, tomato, pickles, and condiments, for serving (optional)

Nutritional Value (Per Serving)

Calories: 500
Protein: 40 g
Fat: 35 g
Carbs: 30 g
Fiber: 2 g
Sugars: 8 g

Directions

1. In a large mixing bowl, combine the ground pork, ground beef, onion, cumin, chili powder, salt, and pepper. Mix well to combine.
2. Divide the mixture into 4 equal portions and shape each portion into a patty.
3. Place the patties on the griddle and cook for 5-6 minutes per side, or until they are cooked to your desired level of doneness.
4. During the last minute of cooking, add a slice of cheese to each patty if using.
5. Place the buns on the griddle, cut side down, and toast for 1-2 minutes, or until they are lightly toasted.
6. Assemble the burgers by placing a patty on the bottom bun and topping it with BBQ sauce, bacon, lettuce, tomato, pickles, and condiments, if desired.
7. Serve the burgers hot, with additional toppings as desired.

TEXAS BURGER WITH BEER CHEESE SAUCE

Made with a mixture of ground beef, spices, and diced onions, and topped with a creamy beer cheese sauce and served on a toasted bun, this burger is sure to become a griddle favorite.

SERVING
4 burgers

PREPARATION
20 min

GRIDDLING TIME
10-15 min

GRIDDLING TEMP
400-425°F

Ingredients

1 1/2 pounds ground beef
1/2 cup diced onion
1 teaspoon ground cumin
1 teaspoon chili powder
1/2 teaspoon salt
1/4 teaspoon black pepper
4 hamburger buns
4 slices cheddar cheese (optional)
1/2 cup beer
2 tablespoons butter
2 tablespoons all-purpose flour
1 cup milk
1/2 cup grated cheddar cheese
Salt and pepper, to taste
Lettuce, tomato, pickles, and condiments, for serving (optional)

Nutritional Value (Per Serving)

Calories: 500
Protein: 30 g
Fat: 35 g
Carbs: 30 g
Fiber: 2 g
Sugars: 4 g

Directions

1. In a large mixing bowl, combine the ground beef, onion, cumin, chili powder, salt, and pepper. Mix well to combine.
2. Divide the mixture into 4 equal portions and shape each portion into a patty.
3. Place the patties on the griddle and cook for 5-6 minutes per side, or until they are cooked to your desired level of doneness.
4. During the last minute of cooking, add a slice of cheese to each patty if using.
5. Place the buns on the griddle, cut side down, and toast for 1-2 minutes, or until they are lightly toasted.
6. While the burgers are cooking, make the beer cheese sauce. In a medium saucepan, melt the butter over medium heat. Add the flour and cook, stirring constantly, for 1-2 minutes, or until the mixture is bubbly and smooth. Slowly add the beer and milk, stirring constantly, until the mixture is smooth and thickened. Add the grated cheddar cheese and stir until it is melted. Season the sauce with salt and pepper, to taste.
7. Assemble the burgers by placing a patty on the bottom bun and topping it with beer cheese sauce, lettuce, tomato, pickles, and condiments, if desired.
8. Serve the burgers hot, with additional toppings as desired.

HOMEMADE VEGGIE BURGER

This Homemade Veggie Burger is made with beans, grains, and vegetables is a delicious and healthy alternative to traditional hamburgers.

SERVING 4 burgers
PREPARATION 30 min
GRIDDLING TIME 10-15 min
GRIDDLING TEMP 400-425°F

Ingredients

1 cup cooked beans (such as black beans, kidney beans, or lentils)
1/2 cup cooked grains (such as quinoa, brown rice, or farro)
1/2 cup grated vegetables (such as carrots, zucchini, or sweet potato)
1/4 cup chopped herbs (such as parsley, cilantro, or basil)
1 egg, beaten
2 tablespoons breadcrumbs
1 teaspoon ground cumin
1 teaspoon chili powder
1/2 teaspoon salt
1/4 teaspoon black pepper
4 hamburger buns
4 slices cheddar cheese (optional)
Lettuce, tomato, pickles, and condiments, for serving (optional)

Nutritional Value (Per Serving)

Calories: 300
Protein: 15 g
Fat: 10 g
Carbs: 45 g
Fiber: 10 g
Sugars: 6 g

Directions

1. In a large mixing bowl, combine the beans, grains, vegetables, herbs, egg, breadcrumbs, cumin, chili powder, salt, and pepper. Mix well to combine.
2. Divide the mixture into 4 equal portions and shape each portion into a patty.
3. Place the patties on the griddle and cook for 5-6 minutes per side, or until they are heated through and lightly browned.
4. During the last minute of cooking, add a slice of cheese to each patty if using.
5. Place the buns on the griddle, cut side down, and toast for 1-2 minutes, or until they are lightly toasted.
6. Assemble the burgers by placing a patty on the bottom bun and topping it with lettuce, tomato, pickles, and condiments, if desired.
7. Serve the burgers hot, with additional toppings as desired.

ST. LOUIS GERBER PORK BURGER

This St. Louis Gerber Pork Burger is a unique and flavorful twist on the classic hamburger. Topped with a spicy sauce and served on a toasted bun, this burger is sure to become a griddle favorite.

SERVING
4 burgers

PREPARATION
20 min

GRIDDLING TIME
10-15 min

GRIDDLING TEMP
400-425°F

Ingredients

- 1 1/2 pounds ground pork
- 1/2 cup diced onion
- 1 teaspoon ground cumin
- 1 teaspoon chili powder
- 1/2 teaspoon salt
- 1/4 teaspoon black pepper
- 4 hamburger buns
- 4 slices pepper jack cheese (optional)
- 1/2 cup mayonnaise
- 1 tablespoon hot sauce
- 2 teaspoons Worcestershire sauce
- 1 teaspoon paprika
- 1/2 teaspoon garlic powder
- Lettuce, tomato, pickles, and condiments, for serving (optional)

Nutritional Value (Per Serving)

- Calories: 500
- Protein: 30 g
- Fat: 35 g
- Carbs: 30 g
- Fiber: 2 g
- Sugars: 4 g

Directions

1. In a large mixing bowl, combine the ground pork, onion, cumin, chili powder, salt, and pepper. Mix well to combine.
2. Divide the mixture into 4 equal portions and shape each portion into a patty.
3. Place the patties on the griddle and cook for 5-6 minutes per side, or until they are cooked to your desired level of doneness.
4. During the last minute of cooking, add a slice of cheese to each patty if using.
5. Place the buns on the griddle, cut side down, and toast for 1-2 minutes, or until they are lightly toasted.
6. While the burgers are cooking, make the sauce by mixing the mayonnaise, hot sauce, Worcestershire sauce, paprika, and garlic powder in a small bowl.
7. Assemble the burgers by placing a patty on the bottom bun and topping it with sauce, lettuce, tomato, pickles, and condiments, if desired.
8. Serve the burgers hot, with additional toppings as desired.

WHITE CHEDDAR TURKEY SMASH BURGER WITH APPLE SLAW

This Smash Burger is made with ground turkey and topped with a creamy apple slaw and is a healthy twist on the classic hamburger.

SERVING: 4 burgers
PREPARATION: 30 min
GRIDDLING TIME: 10-15 min
GRIDDLING TEMP: 400-425°F

Ingredients

1 1/2 pounds ground turkey
1/2 teaspoon salt
1/4 teaspoon black pepper
4 hamburger buns
4 slices white cheddar cheese
1/2 cup mayonnaise
1/4 cup sour cream
2 tablespoons apple cider vinegar
1 teaspoon sugar
1/2 teaspoon celery seed
4 cups shredded cabbage
1 apple, thinly sliced
Lettuce, tomato, pickles, and condiments, for serving (optional)

Nutritional Value (Per Serving)

Calories: 400
Protein: 30 g
Fat: 25 g
Carbs: 30 g
Fiber: 4 g
Sugars: 8 g

Directions

1. In a large mixing bowl, combine the ground turkey, salt, and pepper. Mix well to combine.
2. Divide the mixture into 4 equal portions and shape each portion into a patty.
3. Place the patties on the griddle and cook for 5-6 minutes per side, or until they are cooked to your desired level of doneness.
4. During the last minute of cooking, add a slice of cheese to each patty.
5. Place the buns on the griddle, cut side down, and toast for 1-2 minutes, or until they are lightly toasted.
6. While the burgers are cooking, make the slaw by mixing the mayonnaise, sour cream, apple cider vinegar, sugar, and celery seed in a large bowl. Add the cabbage and apple to the bowl and mix until well coated.
7. Assemble the burgers by placing a patty on the bottom bun and topping it with slaw, lettuce, tomato, pickles, and condiments, if desired.
8. Serve the burgers hot, with additional toppings as desired.

Chapter 03

VEGETABLES & SIDE DISHES

BACON AND CORN GRIDDLE CAKES

Made with a combination of bacon, corn, and flour, these cakes are packed with flavor, but I would recommend you to top them with syrup and give your taste buds and belly a party.

SERVING
8 cakes

PREPARATION
30 min

GRIDDLING TIME
10-15 min

GRIDDLING TEMP
350-375°F

Ingredients

1 cup all-purpose flour
1 cup cornmeal
1 tablespoon sugar
2 teaspoons baking powder
1/2 teaspoon baking soda
1/2 teaspoon salt
1 cup buttermilk
1 egg
2 tablespoons melted butter
1/2 cup cooked and crumbled bacon
1/2 cup canned corn, drained
Cooking spray or butter, for greasing the griddle
Maple syrup and butter, for serving (optional)

Nutritional Value (Per Serving)

Calories: 300
Protein: 10 g
Fat: 15 g
Carbs: 30 g
Fiber: 2 g
Sugars: 8 g

Directions

1. In a large mixing bowl, combine the flour, cornmeal, sugar, baking powder, baking soda, and salt. Mix well to combine.
2. In a separate bowl, whisk together the buttermilk, egg, and melted butter.
3. Add the wet ingredients to the dry ingredients and mix until just combined. Stir in the bacon and corn.
4. Heat the griddle over medium heat and grease it with cooking spray or butter.
5. Use a 1/4 cup measuring cup to scoop the batter onto the griddle. Cook the cakes for 2-3 minutes per side, or until they are golden brown and cooked through.
6. Serve the cakes warm, with maple syrup and butter, if desired.

HIBACHI VEGETABLES

This a delicious and healthy side dish that can be made quickly on a gas griddle. It's sweet and savory and makes a great addition to a dinner party menu.

SERVING
4 people

PREPARATION
20 min

GRIDDLING TIME
15-20 min

GRIDDLING TEMP
400-450°F

Ingredients

1 red bell pepper, sliced
1 yellow bell pepper, sliced
1 onion, sliced
2 cups mushrooms, sliced
2 tablespoons vegetable oil
2 tablespoons soy sauce
2 tablespoons sake (or dry white wine)
1 tablespoon sugar
2 cloves garlic, minced
Salt and pepper, to taste
Green onions, thinly sliced, for garnish (optional)

Nutritional Value (Per Serving)

Calories: 100
Protein: 3 g
Fat: 8 g
Carbs: 7 g
Fiber: 2 g
Sugars: 4 g

Directions

1. In a large mixing bowl, toss the bell peppers, onions, and mushrooms with the vegetable oil, soy sauce, sake, sugar, garlic, salt, and pepper until well coated.
2. Preheat the gas griddle over medium-high heat.
3. Add the vegetables to the griddle and cook, stirring occasionally, until they are tender and lightly charred, about 15-20 minutes.
4. Remove the vegetables from the griddle, place them in a serving dish and garnish with sliced green onions, if desired.
5. Serve the vegetables warm as a side dish to any entree, or with some rice and/or a protein source such as chicken, beef, or shrimp.

GRIDDLE VEGETABLE QUESADILLAS

These griddle vegetables are a delicious and healthy twist on traditional quesadillas. Made with a combination of vegetables, cheese, and tortillas, these quesadillas are packed with flavor and have a crispy, golden-brown exterior. They are perfect for a quick lunch or dinner.

SERVING
4 quesadillas

PREPARATION
20 min

GRIDDLING TIME
10-15 min

GRIDDLING TEMP
400-425°F

Ingredients

4 large flour tortillas
1 cup grated cheese (cheddar, Monterey Jack or a combination)
1 red bell pepper, diced
1 green bell pepper, diced
1 red onion, diced
1 zucchini, diced
1 teaspoon chili powder
1/2 teaspoon cumin
Salt and pepper, to taste
Cooking spray or butter, for greasing the griddle
Sour cream and salsa, for serving (optional)

Nutritional Value (Per Serving)

Calories: 300
Protein: 12 g
Fat: 15 g
Carbs: 25 g
Fiber: 2 g
Sugars: 4 g

Directions

1. Heat the gas griddle to medium-high heat and grease it with cooking spray or butter.
2. In a bowl, mix together the bell peppers, onion, zucchini, chili powder, cumin, salt, and pepper.
3. Place a tortilla on the griddle. Sprinkle a little bit of cheese in the middle of the tortilla then add some of the vegetable mixtures. Sprinkle more cheese over top. Place another tortilla on top of that, and press down a bit to seal it.
4. Cook the quesadilla for 2-3 minutes per side, or until the tortilla is golden brown and the cheese is melted.
5. Repeat with the remaining tortillas, vegetables, and cheese.
6. Cut the quesadillas into wedges and serve warm, with sour cream and salsa, if desired.

MAPLE BACON BRUSSELS SPROUTS

This delicious and unique side dish that can be made quickly on a gas griddle and is one dish that I think everyone needs to experience in their lifetime.

SERVING
4 people

PREPARATION
20 min

GRIDDLING TIME
15-20 min

GRIDDLING TEMP
425-450°F

Ingredients

1 lb. Brussels sprouts, halved
6-8 slices of bacon, cut into small pieces
2 tablespoons olive oil
2 tablespoons maple syrup
Salt and pepper, to taste

Directions

1. Preheat the gas griddle to medium-high heat.
2. In a mixing bowl, toss the Brussels sprouts and bacon with olive oil, maple syrup, salt, and pepper until well coated.
3. Add the mixture to the griddle and cook, stirring occasionally, until the Brussels sprouts are tender and the bacon is crispy about 15-20 minutes.
4. Serve the Brussels sprouts warm as a side dish or as a topping for a salad.

Nutritional Value (Per Serving)

Calories: 180
Protein: 6 g
Fat: 13 g
Carbs: 12 g
Fiber: 4 g
Sugars: 7 g

CRISPY FRIED GREEN TOMATOES

This southern classic is made with green tomatoes that are breaded and fried to perfection, resulting in a crispy exterior and a tangy, juicy interior.

SERVING 4 people	**PREPARATION** 30 min	**GRIDDLING TIME** 15-20 min	**GRIDDLING TEMP** 375-400°F

Ingredients

4-6 green tomatoes, sliced 1/4 inch thick
1/2 cup all-purpose flour
1/2 teaspoon paprika
1/4 teaspoon cayenne pepper
Salt and pepper, to taste
2 eggs, beaten
1 cup breadcrumbs
1 cup cornmeal
Vegetable oil, for frying
Ranch dressing, for serving (optional)

Nutritional Value (Per Serving)

Calories: 260
Protein: 7 g
Fat: 14 g
Carbs: 27 g
Fiber: 3 g
Sugars: 10 g

Directions

1. In a shallow dish, combine the flour, paprika, cayenne pepper, salt, and pepper.
2. In a second shallow dish, beat the eggs.
3. In a third shallow dish, combine the breadcrumbs and cornmeal.
4. Dip the tomato slices in the flour mixture, then the eggs, and then coat them well in the breadcrumb mixture.
5. Heat the oil in the gas griddle to 375-400°F. Carefully place the breaded tomatoes in the griddle and fry them for 2-3 minutes on each side, or until they are golden brown.
6. Remove the tomatoes from the griddle with a slotted spoon and place them on a paper-towel-lined plate to drain.
7. Serve the tomatoes warm with ranch dressing, if desired.

GRIDDLED VEGETABLES WITH MELTING AUBERGINES

This flavorful and healthy dish that is is packed with vitamins, minerals and antioxidants and is perfect for a summer meal or as a side dish.

SERVING 4 people
PREPARATION 15 min
GRIDDLING TIME 15-20 min
GRIDDLING TEMP 375-400°F

Ingredients

1 large aubergine, sliced
1 red pepper, sliced
1 yellow pepper, sliced
1 courgette, sliced
1 red onion, sliced
1 tbsp olive oil
1 tsp smoked paprika
1 tsp dried oregano
1 tsp garlic powder
Salt and pepper, to taste
1 tbsp chopped fresh parsley

Directions

1. Preheat the gas griddle to 375-400°F.
2. In a large bowl, combine the aubergine, red pepper, yellow pepper, courgette, and red onion.
3. Add the olive oil, smoked paprika, oregano, garlic powder, salt, and pepper. Toss the vegetables to coat them evenly.
4. Place the vegetables on the griddle and cook for 8-10 minutes per side or until tender and charred.
5. Remove the vegetables from the griddle and sprinkle them with the fresh parsley.
6. Serve the vegetables hot or at room temperature as a side dish or as a topping for pasta, rice, or quinoa.

Nutritional Value (Per Serving)

Calories: 120
Protein: 2g
Fat: 8g
Carbs: 12g
Fiber: 3g
Sugars: 7g

Chapter 04

BEEF RECIPES

FLASH-MARINATED SKIRT STEAK

This recipe marinates the steak for only a short period of time to add flavor and tenderize the meat.

SERVING 4 people
PREPARATION 15 min
MARINATION 15 min
GRIDDLING TIME 10-15 min
GRIDDLING TEMP 425-450°F

Ingredients

1 1/2 lb. skirt steak
1/4 cup soy sauce
2 tablespoons olive oil
2 cloves of garlic, minced
1 tablespoon brown sugar
1 teaspoon smoked paprika
1/4 teaspoon cayenne pepper
Salt and pepper, to taste

Directions

1. In a shallow dish, mix together the soy sauce, olive oil, garlic, brown sugar, smoked paprika, cayenne pepper, salt, and pepper.
2. Place the steak in the dish and coat it well with the marinade. Allow the steak to marinate for 15 minutes.
3. Heat the gas griddle to 425-450°F.
4. Remove the steak from the marinade and discard the marinade.
5. Place the steak on the griddle and cook it for 4-5 minutes per side, or until it reaches your desired level of doneness.
6. Let the steak rest for 5-10 minutes before slicing it against the grain.
7. Serve the steak with your favorite sides or toppings.

Nutritional Value (Per Serving)

Calories: 330
Protein: 45 g
Fat: 14 g
Carbs: 4 g
Fiber: 1 g
Sugars: 3 g

HOMEMADE MEATBALLS

This recipe for meatballs is made with a combination of ground beef and pork, seasoned with classic Italian herbs and spices, and cooked to perfection on a gas griddle.

SERVING
6 people

PREPARATION
15 min

GRIDDLING TIME
15-20 min

GRIDDLING TEMP
425-450°F

Ingredients

1 lb. ground beef
1 lb. ground pork
1/2 cup breadcrumbs
1/4 cup grated Parmesan cheese
1/4 cup minced onion
2 cloves of garlic, minced
2 eggs
1 tablespoon chopped fresh parsley
1 teaspoon dried basil
1 teaspoon dried oregano
1/2 teaspoon salt
1/4 teaspoon pepper

Directions

1. In a large mixing bowl, combine the ground beef, ground pork, breadcrumbs, Parmesan cheese, onion, garlic, eggs, parsley, basil, oregano, salt, and pepper. Mix until well combined.
2. Shape the mixture into 1 and 1/2-inch meatballs.
3. Heat the gas griddle to 425-450°F.
4. Place the meatballs on the griddle and cook for 10-12 minutes, turning them occasionally, until they are browned and cooked through.
5. Serve the meatballs warm with spaghetti and marinara sauce or in a sandwich or as an appetizer.

Nutritional Value (Per Serving)

Calories: 400
Protein: 25 g
Fat: 29 g
Carbs: 15 g
Fiber: 1 g
Sugars: 2 g

COPYCAT TEXAS ROADHOUSE STEAK

This copycat recipe captures the bold flavors of the steaks served at Texas Roadhouse restaurants. It's a juicy, flavorful steak that is sure to satisfy any steak lover.

SERVING 4 people | **PREPARATION** 15 min | **MARINATION** 15 min | **GRIDDLING TIME** 10-15 min | **GRIDDLING TEMP** 425-450°F

Ingredients

4 (8-ounce) beef steaks (such as ribeye, sirloin, or New York strip)
2 tablespoons paprika
2 tablespoons brown sugar
2 tablespoons salt
1 tablespoon black pepper
1 tablespoon garlic powder
1 tablespoon onion powder
1 tablespoon dried thyme
1 teaspoon cayenne pepper
2 tablespoons vegetable oil

Nutritional Value (Per Serving)

Calories: 600
Protein: 60g
Fat: 40g
Carbs: 10g
Fiber: 3g
Sugars: 5g

Directions

1. Mix together the paprika, brown sugar, salt, pepper, garlic powder, onion powder, thyme, and cayenne pepper in a small bowl.
2. Rub the mixture all over the steaks and let them sit at room temperature for 15 minutes.
3. Heat the oil on the gas griddle to 425-450°F.
4. Place the steaks on the griddle and cook them for 4-5 minutes per side, or until they reach your desired level of doneness.
5. Remove the steaks from the griddle and let them rest for 5-10 minutes before slicing and serving.

GRIDDLE STEAK BITES

These steak bites are marinated in a flavorful mix of soy sauce, brown sugar, garlic, and spices before they are cooked on a hot gas griddle.

SERVING 6 people
PREPARATION 10 min
MARINATION 2 hrs
GRIDDLING TIME 8-10 min
GRIDDLING TEMP 425-450°F

Ingredients

2 lbs. sirloin steak, cut into 1-inch cubes
1/2 cup soy sauce
1/4 cup brown sugar
2 cloves of garlic, minced
1 teaspoon smoked paprika
1/2 teaspoon onion powder
1/4 teaspoon black pepper
1/4 teaspoon cayenne pepper
Vegetable oil, for frying

Directions

1. In a large bowl, mix together the soy sauce, brown sugar, garlic, smoked paprika, onion powder, black pepper, and cayenne pepper.
2. Add the steak cubes to the marinade and toss to coat. Cover and refrigerate for at least 2 hours.
3. Heat the oil on the gas griddle to 425-450°F.
4. Drain the steak from the marinade and discard the marinade.
5. Carefully place the steak bites on the griddle and cook them for 2-3 minutes per side, or until they are browned and cooked through.
6. Remove the steak bites from the griddle and let them rest for a few minutes before serving.

Nutritional Value (Per Serving)

Calories: 480
Protein: 50g
Fat: 24g
Carbs: 12g
Fiber: 1g
Sugars: 8g

GRILLED BEEF TENDERLOIN WITH HERB-GARLIC-PEPPER COATING

This recipe for Grilled Beef Tenderloin with Herb-Garlic-Pepper Coating is a delicious way to enjoy a tender and juicy cut of beef.

SERVING 6 people
PREPARATION 15 min
MARINATION 2 hrs
GRIDDLING TIME 20-25 min
GRIDDLING TEMP 425-450°F

Ingredients

2 lbs. beef tenderloin, trimmed
2 cloves of garlic, minced
2 tablespoons olive oil
1 tablespoon fresh rosemary, finely chopped
1 tablespoon fresh thyme, finely chopped
1 tablespoon fresh parsley, finely chopped
1 teaspoon salt
1/2 teaspoon black pepper
additional oil for griddling

Nutritional Value (Per Serving)

Calories: 400
Protein: 40g
Fat: 20g
Carbs: 2g
Fiber: 1g
Sugars: 0g

Directions

1. In a small bowl, mix together the garlic, olive oil, rosemary, thyme, parsley, salt, and pepper.
2. Rub the mixture all over the beef tenderloin, cover, and refrigerate for at least 2 hours.
3. Heat the oil on the gas griddle to 425-450°F.
4. Place the beef tenderloin on the griddle and cook it for 10-12 minutes per side or until it reaches the desired level of doneness.
5. Remove the beef tenderloin from the griddle and let it rest for 5-10 minutes before slicing and serving.

SIRLOIN WRAPPED JALAPEÑO POPPERS

This is a fun and flavorful way to enjoy jalapeño poppers, with a juicy and tender sirloin steak wrapping them, with a cream filling.

SERVING
8 people

PREPARATION
20 min

GRIDDLING TIME
15-20 min

GRIDDLING TEMP
425-450°F

Ingredients

8 jalapeño peppers, halved and seeded
8 oz cream cheese, softened
8 strips of bacon, sliced in half
8 sirloin steaks, pounded thin
Salt and pepper, to taste
Vegetable oil, for griddling

Nutritional Value (Per Serving)

Calories: 550
Protein: 45g
Fat: 40g
Carbs: 5g
Fiber: 1g
Sugars: 3g

Directions

1. Preheat the gas griddle to 425-450°F.
2. In a bowl, mix together the cream cheese with salt and pepper to taste.
3. Stuff the jalapeño halves with the cream cheese mixture.
4. Wrap a half strip of bacon around each jalapeño popper and secure it with a toothpick.
5. Place the poppers on the griddle and cook them for 8-10 minutes or until the bacon is crispy and the poppers are heated through.
6. Season the sirloin steaks with salt and pepper, then griddle them to your desired doneness.
7. Carefully wrap the steak around the jalapeño popper and toothpick it to secure it.
8. Griddle the wrapped poppers for 2-3 minutes on each side, or until the steak is browned and cooked through.

Chapter 05

PORK RECIPES

PERFECT PORK CHOPS

The pork chops are seasoned with garlic, thyme, and rosemary, then grilled to perfection and if you want to add some extra flavor you can add some marinade. Get creative!

SERVING
4 people

PREPARATION
15 min

GRIDDLING TIME
8-10 min

GRIDDLING TEMP
425-450°F

Ingredients

4 bone-in pork chops, about 1-inch thick
Salt and pepper, to taste
2 cloves of garlic, minced
1 tbsp olive oil
1 tsp dried thyme
1 tsp dried rosemary

Directions

1. Preheat the gas griddle to 425-450°F.
2. Season the pork chops with salt, pepper, minced garlic, thyme, and rosemary.
3. Brush the pork chops with olive oil on both sides.
4. Place the pork chops on the griddle and cook them for 4-5 minutes per side or until the internal temperature reaches 145°F.
5. Let the pork chops rest for 5 minutes before slicing or serving.

Nutritional Value (Per Serving)

Calories: 340
Protein: 40g
Fat: 25g
Carbs: 1g
Fiber: 0g
Sugars: 0g

SMOKY GRILLED PORK CHOPS

The marinade with brown sugar, smoked paprika, garlic powder, and apple cider vinegar gives the pork a special flavor, and grilling gives the pork a crispy exterior while keeping it moist inside.

SERVING
4 people

PREPARATION
30 min

GRIDDLING TIME
8-10 min

GRIDDLING TEMP
425-450°F

Ingredients

4 bone-in pork chops, about 1-inch thick
1/4 cup brown sugar
2 tablespoons smoked paprika
1 tablespoon garlic powder
1 teaspoon salt
1 teaspoon black pepper
1/4 cup olive oil
1/4 cup apple cider vinegar

Nutritional Value (Per Serving)

Calories: 400
Protein: 40g
Fat: 25g
Carbs: 15g
Fiber: 1g
Sugars: 13g

Directions

1. In a small bowl, mix together brown sugar, smoked paprika, garlic powder, salt, and pepper.
2. In another small bowl, mix together the olive oil and apple cider vinegar.
3. Place the pork chops in a shallow dish and pour the marinade over them, making sure to coat them evenly. Cover and refrigerate for at least 2 hours or overnight for best results.
4. Preheat the gas griddle to 425-450°F.
5. Remove the pork chops from the marinade and let any excess marinade drip off.
6. Place the pork chops on the griddle and cook them for 4-5 minutes per side or until the internal temperature reaches 145°F.
7. Let the pork chops rest for 5 minutes before slicing or serving.

MARINATED PORK SKEWERS

Marinating the pork in a mixture of soy sauce, brown sugar, garlic, ginger, sesame oil, and red pepper flakes, and grilling the skewers will give it a nice crust on the outside and juicy on the inside.

SERVING	PREPARATION	GRIDDLING TIME	GRIDDLING TEMP
4 people	30 min	10-12 min	425-450°F

Ingredients

1 lb pork tenderloin, cut into 1-inch cubes
1/4 cup soy sauce
1/4 cup brown sugar
2 cloves of garlic, minced
1 tbsp olive oil
1 tsp ground ginger
1 tsp sesame oil
1/4 tsp red pepper flakes (optional)
wooden skewers (soaked in water for at least 30 minutes before using)

Nutritional Value (Per Serving)

Calories: 200
Protein: 20g
Fat: 10g
Carbs: 12g
Fiber: 0g
Sugars: 10g

Directions

1. In a small bowl, mix together soy sauce, brown sugar, minced garlic, olive oil, ground ginger, sesame oil, and red pepper flakes (if using).
2. Place the pork cubes in a shallow dish and pour the marinade over them, making sure to coat them evenly. Cover and refrigerate for at least 2 hours, or overnight for best results.
3. Preheat the gas griddle to 425-450°F.
4. Thread the pork cubes onto the skewers, leaving a little space between each piece.
5. Place the skewers on the griddle and cook them for 5-6 minutes per side, or until the pork is cooked through and the internal temperature reaches 145°F.
6. Let the skewers rest for a few minutes before serving.

GRIDDLED PORK AND PEACHES

This recipe gives you a combination of sweet and savory flavors, by marinating the pork medallions with honey, Dijon mustard and thyme, and then griddle it.

SERVING 4 people

PREPARATION 20 min

GRIDDLING TIME 8-10 min

GRIDDLING TEMP 425-450°F

Ingredients

1 lb pork tenderloin, sliced into 1/2-inch thick medallions
Salt and pepper, to taste
2 tbsp olive oil
4 ripe peaches, cut into wedges
1 tbsp honey
1 tsp Dijon mustard
1 tbsp chopped fresh thyme

Directions

1. Season the pork medallions with salt and pepper on both sides.
2. Heat the olive oil in a gas griddle over medium-high heat. Add the pork medallions and cook for 4-5 minutes per side or until the internal temperature reaches 145°F.
3. Remove the pork from the griddle and set it aside to rest.
4. In the same griddle, add the peach wedges, honey, Dijon mustard, and thyme. Cook for 2-3 minutes or until the peaches are slightly softened and caramelized.
5. Serve the pork medallions with the peaches on top and enjoy!

Nutritional Value (Per Serving)

Calories: 300
Protein: 30g
Fat: 15g
Carbs: 15g
Fiber: 3g
Sugars: 12g

GRIDDLE PORK FRIED RICE

The pork is seasoned with salt and pepper and cooked on a gas griddle until and then mixed with onions, garlic, cooked rice, soy sauce, eggs, frozen peas and carrots, and green onions–this dish can't go wrong.

SERVING
4 people

PREPARATION
20 min

GRIDDLING TIME
15-20 min

GRIDDLING TEMP
425-450°F

Ingredients

1 lb pork tenderloin, diced
1 tsp salt
1 tsp pepper
1 tbsp vegetable oil
1 onion, diced
2 cloves of garlic, minced
2 cups cooked white rice
1/4 cup soy sauce
2 eggs, beaten
1 cup frozen peas and carrots
2 green onions, sliced

Nutritional Value (Per Serving)

Calories: 400
Protein: 30g
Fat: 15g
Carbs: 40g
Fiber: 3g
Sugars: 3g

Directions

1. Season the pork with salt and pepper.
2. Heat the vegetable oil in a gas griddle over medium-high heat. Add the pork and cook for 6-8 minutes or until the internal temperature reaches 145°F.
3. Remove the pork from the griddle and set it aside.
4. In the same griddle, add the onion and garlic and cook until softened.
5. Add the cooked rice, soy sauce, eggs, peas and carrots, and green onions. Cook for an additional 3-4 minutes, or until the eggs are fully cooked.
6. Add the pork back to the griddle, and cook for 1-2 minutes to heat it through.

SIMPLE SMOKED PULLED PORK BUTT

This recipe allows you to achieve that traditional barbecue style pulled pork, by smoking it on a gas griddle, which allows the pork to cook until it's perfectly tender and juicy.

SERVING	PREPARATION	SMOKING	GRIDDLING TIME	GRIDDLING TEMP
8 people	20 min	3-4 hrs	2-3 hrs	250-275°F

Ingredients

1 (8-10 lb) pork butt
1 cup of your favorite BBQ rub
1 cup of apple juice

Directions

1. Trim any excess fat from the pork butt.
2. Rub the pork butt evenly with the BBQ rub.
3. Place the pork butt in a large aluminum pan and pour apple juice over it.
4. Cover the pan with foil and let it sit in the refrigerator for at least 4 hours or overnight for best results.
5. Preheat your gas griddle to 250-275°F.
6. Place the pork butt on the griddle and smoke it with your preferred smoking wood for 3-4 hours or until the internal temperature reaches 205°F.
7. Smoking on a gas griddle is more challenging than using a traditional smoker, and will not produce the same level of smoke flavor and complexity that you can get from traditional smoking (it is also important to make sure that you're using a gas griddle that is capable of handling the low temperatures and that can hold the wood chips, or a smoke box if possible). But here is how you can smoke using a griddle.
    a. Add wood chips or chunks: You will need to add wood chips or chunks to the griddle in order to achieve a smoky flavor. Soak the wood chips in water for at least 30 minutes before adding them to the griddle.
    b. Create a smoke box: You can create a smoke box by placing the soaked wood chips in a foil pouch and then placing the pouch on the griddle. This will allow the wood chips to smoke without catching fire.
    c. Keep the griddle closed: Try to keep the lid of the griddle closed as much as possible to trap the smoke inside and give your food a chance to absorb the smoky flavor.
    d. Lower the temperature: It's important to keep the temperature low and steady, around 250-275°F, during the smoking process. This will help ensure that the meat cooks slowly and has a chance to absorb the smoke flavor.
    e. Add a thermometer: Keep an eye on the internal temperature of your meat to ensure it reaches the desired level of doneness.
8. Remove the pork from the griddle and let it rest for 30 minutes.
9. Shred the pork with two forks or meat claws and serve with your favorite BBQ sauce.

Nutritional Value (Per Serving)

Calories: 450
Protein: 50g
Fat: 30g
Carbs: 5g
Fiber: 1g
Sugars: 3g

Chapter 06

CHICKEN RECIPES

SEARED CHICKEN BREASTS

This is a simple and easy recipe for juicy and flavorful chicken breasts. The searing will give you a nice crust on the outside while keeping the chicken moist inside.

SERVING
4 people

PREPARATION
10 min

GRIDDLING TIME
6-8 min

GRIDDLING TEMP
425–450°F

Ingredients

4 boneless, skinless chicken breasts
1 tsp salt
1 tsp pepper
1 tbsp olive oil

Directions

1. Season both sides of the chicken breasts with salt and pepper.
2. Heat the olive oil in a gas griddle over medium-high heat.
3. Place the chicken breasts on the griddle and cook for 3-4 minutes per side, or until the internal temperature reaches 165°F.
4. Remove the chicken from the griddle and let it rest for a few minutes before serving.

Nutritional Value (Per Serving)

Calories: 200
Protein: 30g
Fat: 8g
Carbs: 0g
Fiber: 0g
Sugars: 0g

CHICKEN TERIYAKI

This recipe for Chicken Teriyaki is a classic Japanese dish with a sweet soy sauce marinade. It's simple and elegant, it's Japanese food.

SERVING
4 people

PREPARATION
10 min

GRIDDLING TIME
6-8 min

GRIDDLING TEMP
425-450°F

Ingredients

4 boneless, skinless chicken breasts
1/2 cup soy sauce
1/2 cup mirin (Japanese sweet rice wine)
1/4 cup sake (optional)
1/4 cup brown sugar
1 tbsp grated ginger
1 tsp minced garlic
1 tbsp vegetable oil
1 green onion, thinly sliced (for garnish)
1 tbsp corn starch dissolved in 1 tbsp cold water

Nutritional Value (Per Serving)

Calories: 250
Protein: 30g
Fat: 10g
Carbs: 15g
Fiber: 1g
Sugars: 12g

Directions

1. In a bowl, mix together the soy sauce, mirin, sake (if using), brown sugar, ginger, and garlic.
2. Place the chicken breasts in a large resealable plastic bag and pour the marinade over the chicken. Seal the bag and toss to evenly coat the chicken. Marinate in the refrigerator for at least 2 hours, or overnight for best results.
3. Heat the vegetable oil in a gas griddle over medium-high heat.
4. Remove the chicken from the marinade, shaking off any excess liquid. Place the chicken on the griddle and discard the remaining marinade.
5. Cook the chicken for 3-4 minutes per side, or until the internal temperature reaches 165°F.
6. While the chicken is cooking, reduce the marinade in a small saucepan over medium-high heat. Once it comes to a boil, reduce heat to low and slowly pour the cornstarch mixture in, whisking constantly, until the sauce thickens.
7. Once the chicken is done, remove it from the griddle, place it on a plate or cutting board and let it rest for a few minutes.
8. Drizzle the thickened sauce over the chicken.
9. Garnish with green onion and serve with rice.

CHICKEN FRIED RICE

The chicken is griddled, then set aside and later tossed in with the fried rice mixture made with onion, garlic, soy sauce, eggs, peas, carrots, and green onions. Can't go wrong with this one.

SERVING 4 people

PREPARATION 10 min

GRIDDLING TIME 6-8 min

GRIDDLING TEMP 425-450°F

Ingredients

1 lb boneless, skinless chicken breasts, diced
1 tsp salt
1 tsp pepper
1 tbsp vegetable oil
1 onion, diced
2 cloves of garlic, minced
2 cups cooked white rice
1/4 cup soy sauce
2 eggs, beaten
1 cup frozen peas and carrots
2 green onions, sliced

Nutritional Value (Per Serving)

Calories: 400
Protein: 30g
Fat: 15g
Carbs: 40g
Fiber: 3g
Sugars: 3g

Directions

1. Season the chicken with salt and pepper.
2. Heat the vegetable oil in a gas griddle over medium-high heat. Add the chicken and cook for 6-8 minutes or until the internal temperature reaches 165°F.
3. Remove the chicken from the griddle and set it aside.
4. In the same griddle, add the onion and garlic and cook until softened.
5. Add the cooked rice, soy sauce, eggs, peas and carrots, and green onions. Cook for an additional 3-4 minutes, or until the eggs are fully cooked.
6. Add the chicken back to the griddle, and cook for 1-2 minutes to heat it through.

PERFECT CHICKEN WINGS

The wings are griddled and then tossed in your favorite wing sauce, making it a healthier option compared to deep-frying.

SERVING
4 people

PREPARATION
10 min

GRIDDLING TIME
15-20 min

GRIDDLING TEMP
425-450°F

Ingredients

2 lb chicken wings
1 tsp salt
1 tsp black pepper
1 tbsp vegetable oil
Your favorite wing sauce

Directions

1. Season the chicken wings with salt and pepper.
2. Heat the vegetable oil on a gas griddle over medium-high heat.
3. Place the wings on the griddle and cook for 8-10 minutes per side or until the internal temperature reaches 165°F.
4. Remove the wings from the griddle and toss them in your favorite wing sauce.
5. Return the wings to the griddle and cook for an additional 2-3 minutes, or until the sauce is heated through and the wings are glazed.

Nutritional Value (Per Serving)

Calories: 400
Protein: 25g
Fat: 30g
Carbs: 10g
Fiber: 1g
Sugars: 8g

CHICKEN LO MEIN

This recipe is a classic Chinese dish that is easy to make on a gas griddle, the chicken is cooked on the griddle, then set aside and later added back to the dish.

SERVING
4 people

PREPARATION
20 min

GRIDDLING TIME
15-20 min

GRIDDLING TEMP
425-450°F

Ingredients

8 oz boneless, skinless chicken breasts, sliced
1/2 tsp salt
1/4 tsp pepper
1 tbsp vegetable oil
1 onion, sliced
1 bell pepper, sliced
1 cup sliced mushrooms
2 cloves of garlic, minced
2 cups cooked lo mein noodles
1/4 cup soy sauce
1/4 cup oyster sauce
1 tbsp rice vinegar
1 tsp sesame oil
2 green onions, sliced

Nutritional Value (Per Serving)

Calories: 400
Protein: 20g
Fat: 15g
Carbs: 40g
Fiber: 2g
Sugars: 5g

Directions

1. Season the chicken with salt and pepper.
2. Heat the vegetable oil in a gas griddle over medium-high heat. Add the chicken and cook for 6-8 minutes or until the internal temperature reaches 165°F.
3. Remove the chicken from the griddle and set it aside.
4. On the same griddle, add the onion, bell pepper, mushrooms, and garlic. Cook until softened.
5. Add the cooked noodles, soy sauce, oyster sauce, rice vinegar, and sesame oil. Stir fry for an additional 2-3 minutes.
6. Add the chicken back to the griddle, and cook for 1-2 minutes to heat it through.
7. Serve the Lo Mein in bowls, garnished with green onions, and enjoy!

CHICKEN WITH MUSHROOM GRAVY

The dish is made with chicken, sautéed onion, mushrooms, garlic and thickened with a mixture of chicken broth and cornstarch with a touch of cream. It's a warm and hearty meal.

SERVING 4 people
PREPARATION 15 min
GRIDDLING TIME 15-20 min
GRIDDLING TEMP 425-450°F

Ingredients

4 boneless, skinless chicken breasts
1 tsp salt
1 tsp pepper
1 tbsp vegetable oil
1 onion, sliced
8 oz sliced mushrooms
2 cloves of garlic, minced
1 cup chicken broth
2 tbsp cornstarch
1/4 cup heavy cream
1 tbsp chopped fresh parsley (for garnish)

Nutritional Value (Per Serving)

Calories: 300
Protein: 30g
Fat: 20g
Carbs: 7g
Fiber: 1g
Sugars: 3g

Directions

1. Season both sides of the chicken breasts with salt and pepper.
2. Heat the vegetable oil in a gas griddle over medium-high heat.
3. Place the chicken breasts on the griddle and cook for 6-8 minutes per side or until the internal temperature reaches 165°F.
4. Remove the chicken from the griddle and set it aside.
5. On the same griddle, add the onion, mushrooms, and garlic. Cook until softened.
6. In a small bowl, mix together the chicken broth and cornstarch.
7. Add the broth mixture and heavy cream to the griddle and stir until the sauce thickens.
8. Add the chicken back to the griddle and spoon the gravy over the top. Cook for an additional 1-2 minutes or until the chicken is heated through.
9. Serve the chicken with the gravy and garnish with parsley.

Chapter 07

POULTRY RECIPES

HERB ROASTED TURKEY

The turkey is seasoned with a blend of herbs and cooked to perfection in the griddle, which results in a juicy and flavorful turkey that is perfect for a special occasion or holiday meal.

SERVING 8-10 people
PREPARATION 15 min
GRIDDLING TIME 2-3 hrs
GRIDDLING TEMP 350-375°F

Ingredients

1 (12-14 lb) turkey, thawed and giblets removed
1 tbsp olive oil
1 tsp salt
1 tsp black pepper
1 tbsp chopped fresh rosemary
1 tbsp chopped fresh thyme
1 tbsp chopped fresh sage
1 onion, cut into wedges
2 cloves of garlic, minced
2 cups chicken broth

Nutritional Value (Per Serving)

Calories: 400
Protein: 30g
Fat: 15g
Carbs: 0g
Fiber: 0g
Sugars: 0g

Directions

1. Preheat the gas griddle to 350-375°F.
2. Rinse the turkey and pat it dry with paper towels.
3. In a small bowl, mix together the olive oil, salt, pepper, rosemary, thyme, and sage.
4. Rub the herb mixture all over the turkey.
5. Place the turkey on the griddle and add the onion and garlic.
6. Pour the chicken broth over the turkey.
7. Close the lid and cook the turkey for 2-3 hours or until the internal temperature reaches 165°F in the thickest part of the turkey.
8. Remove the turkey from the griddle and let it rest for at least 20 minutes before carving.

MARINATED SMOKED TURKEY BREAST

The turkey is seasoned with salt, pepper, and BBQ rub and cooked using the indirect grilling method, which means the turkey is placed away from the heat source and the lid is closed.

SERVING
8 people

PREPARATION
8 hrs

GRIDDLING TIME
1.5-2 hrs

GRIDDLING TEMP
225-250°F

Ingredients

1 (6-8 lb) turkey breast, thawed and giblets removed
1 cup of your favorite marinade
1 tbsp vegetable oil
1 tsp salt
1 tsp pepper
1 tbsp your favorite BBQ rub

Nutritional Value (Per Serving)

Calories: 250
Protein: 40g
Fat: 10g
Carbs: 2g
Fiber: 0g
Sugars: 2g

Directions

1. In a large resealable bag, combine your favorite marinade and turkey breast. Seal the bag, and refrigerate for at least 8 hours or overnight for best results.
2. Preheat the gas griddle to 225-250°F and set it up for indirect grilling.
3. Remove the turkey breast from the marinade and pat it dry with paper towels.
4. Brush the turkey breast with vegetable oil and season with salt, pepper, and BBQ rub.
5. Place the turkey breast on the griddle, away from the heat source and close the lid.
6. Cook the turkey breast for 1.5-2 hours or until the internal temperature reaches 165°F.
7. Remove the turkey breast from the griddle, and let it rest for at least 15 minutes before slicing and serving.

BRINED GRILLED TURKEY WITH MAPLE BOURBON GLAZE

This dish is filled with nutrients and in addition, the maple syrup, brown sugar and soy sauce make it a sweet and savoury delight.

SERVING
8-10 people

PREPARATION
12 hrs

GRIDDLING TIME
2-3 hrs

GRIDDLING TEMP
350-375°F

Ingredients

1 (12-14 lb) turkey, thawed & giblets removed

For the brine:
2 gallons water
1 cup kosher salt
1 cup maple syrup
1 cup brown sugar
1 cup soy sauce
1 cup bourbon
1 tbsp black peppercorns
1 tbsp juniper berries
1 tbsp chopped fresh rosemary
1 tbsp chopped fresh thyme
1 tbsp chopped fresh sage
1 onion, cut into wedges
2 cloves of garlic, minced

For the glaze:
1/2 cup maple syrup
1/4 cup bourbon
1 tbsp Dijon mustard
1 tsp chopped fresh rosemary
1 tsp chopped fresh thyme
1 tsp chopped fresh sage

Nutritional Value (Per Serving)

Caloric content: 400-500 calories
Protein: 30-35 grams
Fat: 20-25 grams
Carbohydrates: 20-25 grams
Fiber: 1-2 grams
Sugar: 15-20 grams
Sodium: 600-700 mg

Directions

1. In a large pot, combine the water, kosher salt, maple syrup, brown sugar, soy sauce, bourbon, peppercorns, juniper berries, rosemary, thyme, and sage. Bring the mixture to a boil, then remove it from the heat and let it cool to room temperature.
2. Place the turkey in a large brining bag or a large pot and pour the cooled brine over the turkey. Seal the bag or cover the pot and refrigerate for at least 12 hours or overnight.
3. Preheat the gas griddle to 350-375°F.
4. Remove the turkey from the brine and pat it dry with paper towels.
5. In a small pot, combine the maple syrup, bourbon, mustard, rosemary, thyme, and sage. Bring the mixture to a simmer and cook for 2-3 minutes or until thickened.
6. Place the turkey on the griddle and brush it with the glaze. Close the lid and cook the turkey for 2-3 hours or until the internal temperature reaches 165°F in the thickest part of the turkey.
7. Remove the turkey from the griddle and let it rest for at least 20 minutes before serving.

Chapter 08

LAMB RECIPES

GRIDDLED LAMB WITH SPICED NEW POTATOES

The lamb is seasoned with a flavorful spice blend, while the new potatoes are tossed with the same spice blend and cooked along the lamb to make a satisfying and well-rounded meal.

SERVING
4 people

PREPARATION
15 min

GRIDDLING TIME
15-20 min

GRIDDLING TEMP
400-450°F

Ingredients

For the lamb:
1 lb lamb leg steaks
1 tsp ground cumin
1 tsp ground coriander
1 tsp ground turmeric
1 tsp smoked paprika
1 tsp salt
1 tsp black pepper
1 tbsp olive oil

For the potatoes:
1 lb new potatoes washed and halved
1 tbsp olive oil
1 tsp ground cumin
1 tsp ground coriander
1 tsp ground turmeric
1 tsp smoked paprika
1 tsp salt
1 tsp black pepper

Nutritional Value (Per Serving)

Caloric content: 350-400 calories
Protein: 30-35 grams
Fat: 15-20 grams
Carbohydrates: 30-35 grams
Fiber: 5 grams
Sugar: 2 grams
Vitamin B12: good source
Iron: good source
Zinc: good source
Vitamin B6: good source
Vitamin C: good source
Potassium: good source

Directions

1. Preheat the gas griddle to 400-450°F.
2. In a small bowl, mix together the cumin, coriander, turmeric, paprika, salt, and pepper.
3. Rub the lamb steaks with the spice mixture and olive oil.
4. In another small bowl, mix together the cumin, coriander, turmeric, paprika, salt, and pepper. Toss the potatoes with the mixture and olive oil.
5. Place the lamb steaks and potatoes on the griddle and cook for 7-8 minutes on each side or until the lamb is cooked to your desired doneness and the potatoes are browned and tender.
6. Serve the lamb steaks and spiced potatoes hot.

GARLIC BUTTER LAMB CHOPS

This is a delicious and easy-to-make recipe that is perfect for a special occasion or a weeknight dinner. The recipe can be easily made on a gas griddle.

SERVING	PREPARATION	GRIDDLING TIME	GRIDDLING TEMP
4 people	10 min	10-15 min	400-450°F

Ingredients

8 lamb chops
4 cloves of garlic, minced
4 tbsp butter, melted
1 tsp chopped fresh rosemary
1 tsp chopped fresh thyme
1 tsp salt
1 tsp black pepper

Directions

1. Preheat the gas griddle to 400-450°F.
2. In a small bowl, mix together the garlic, butter, rosemary, thyme, salt, and pepper.
3. Brush the lamb chops with the butter mixture.
4. Place the lamb chops on the griddle and cook for 4-5 minutes on each side or until they are cooked to your desired doneness.
5. Serve the lamb chops hot.

Nutritional Value (Per Serving)

Caloric content: 450-500 calories
Protein: 30-35 grams
Fat: 40-45 grams
Carbohydrates: 2-5 grams
Fiber: 0 grams
Sugar: 0 grams
Cholesterol: 120-140 mg
Saturated Fat: 20-25 grams

GARLIC & ROSEMARY GRILLED LAMB CHOPS

The lamb chops are marinated in a flavorful garlic and rosemary mixture, which infuses the meat with a rich, herbaceous flavor.

SERVING
4 people

PREPARATION
20 min

GRIDDLING TIME
8-10 min

GRIDDLING TEMP
425-450°F

Ingredients

8 lamb chops
4 cloves of garlic, minced
4 tbsp butter, melted
1 tsp chopped fresh rosemary
1 tsp chopped fresh thyme
1 tsp salt
1 tsp black pepper

Directions

1. In a small bowl, mix together the garlic, olive oil, rosemary, salt, and pepper.
2. Rub the mixture all over the lamb chops, making sure to coat them evenly.
3. Cover the chops and refrigerate for at least 30 minutes or overnight
4. Preheat the gas griddle to 425-450°F.
5. Remove the lamb chops from the marinade and shake off any excess marinade.
6. Place the lamb chops on the griddle and cook for 4-5 minutes on each side or until they are cooked to your desired doneness.
7. Serve the lamb chops hot.

Nutritional Value (Per Serving)

Caloric content: 250-300 calories
Protein: 25-30 grams
Fat: 20-25 grams
Carbohydrates: 0-2 grams
Fiber: 0 grams
Sugar: 0 grams

Chapter 09

WILD GAME RECIPES

SWEET JALAPENO GRILLED DUCK

This is a delicious and easy-to-make recipe that is perfect for a special occasion or a weeknight dinner. The recipe can be easily made on a gas griddle.

SERVING
4 people

PREPARATION
10 min

GRIDDLING TIME
10-15 min

GRIDDLING TEMP
400-450°F

Ingredients

4 duck breasts
1/2 cup brown sugar
1/4 cup soy sauce
2 tbsp honey
2 tbsp rice vinegar
1 tbsp grated ginger
1 tbsp grated garlic
1 jalapeno pepper, seeded and diced
Salt and pepper, to taste

Directions

1. In a small bowl, mix together the brown sugar, soy sauce, honey, rice vinegar, ginger, garlic, jalapeno pepper, salt, and pepper.
2. Place the duck breasts in a shallow dish and pour the marinade over the top. Make sure the duck is well coated.
3. Cover the dish and refrigerate for at least 1 hour or overnight.
4. Preheat the gas griddle to 400-450°F.
5. Remove the duck breasts from the marinade and shake off any excess marinade.
6. Place the duck breasts on the griddle and cook for 6-8 minutes per side or until they are cooked to your desired doneness.
7. Serve the duck breasts hot with the marinade as a sauce.

Nutritional Value (Per Serving)

Caloric content: 250-300 calories
Protein: 25-30 grams
Fat: 20-25 grams
Carbohydrates: 15-20 grams
Fiber: 0 grams
Sugar: 12-15 grams

GRILLED VENISON STEAK WITH BALSAMIC MOREL SAUCE

This is a delicious and unique recipe that is perfect for a special occasion or a weeknight dinner.

SERVING
4 people

PREPARATION
20 min

GRIDDLING TIME
8-10 min

GRIDDLING TEMP
425-450°F

Ingredients

4 venison steaks
1 tsp salt
1 tsp black pepper
1 tbsp olive oil

Sauce:
1 cup morel mushrooms, sliced
1 shallot, minced
1 clove of garlic, minced
1/4 cup balsamic vinegar
1/4 cup beef broth
2 tbsp butter
1 tsp chopped fresh thyme
1 tsp chopped fresh rosemary
Salt and pepper, to taste

Nutritional Value (Per Serving)

Caloric content: 200-250 calories
Protein: 25-30 grams
Fat: 10-12 grams
Carbohydrates: 5-7 grams
Fiber: 1-2 grams
Sugar: 3-5 grams

Directions

1. Preheat the gas griddle to 425-450°F.
2. Season the venison steaks with salt and pepper, then brush them with olive oil.
3. Place the steaks on the griddle and cook for 4-5 minutes per side or until they are cooked to your desired doneness.
4. Remove the steaks from the griddle and let them rest for a few minutes.
5. In a pan, sauté the morel mushrooms, shallot, and garlic until the mushrooms are tender.
6. Add the balsamic vinegar, beef broth, butter, thyme, rosemary, salt, and pepper to the pan and bring to a simmer.
7. Let the sauce reduce for a few minutes until it thickens.
8. Serve the venison steaks with the balsamic morel sauce on top.

BACON WRAPPED VENISON

This recipe takes advantage of the rich and gamey flavor of venison, which is paired with the salty and smoky flavor of bacon.

SERVING: 4 people
PREPARATION: 20 min
GRIDDLING TIME: 10-12 min
GRIDDLING TEMP: 425-450°F

Ingredients

- 4 venison steaks
- 4 slices of bacon
- 1 tsp salt
- 1 tsp black pepper
- 1 tbsp olive oil

Directions

1. Preheat the gas griddle to 425-450°F.
2. Season the venison steaks with salt and pepper, then brush them with olive oil.
3. Wrap each venison steak with a slice of bacon and secure it with toothpicks.
4. Place the steaks on the griddle and cook for 5-6 minutes per side or until they are cooked to your desired doneness.
5. Remove the steaks from the griddle and let them rest for a few minutes.
6. Serve the venison steaks hot, with the bacon still wrapped around them.

Nutritional Value (Per Serving)

Caloric content: 400-450 calories
Protein: 25-30 grams
Fat: 25-30 grams
Carbohydrates: 1-2 grams
Fiber: 0 grams
Sugar: 0 grams
Cholesterol: 75-100 mg

ROASTED DUCK BREAST

The recipe takes advantage of the rich flavor of duck, which is paired with the sweetness of honey and the earthy flavor of thyme to give out a dish that deserves to be on a fine dine menu.

SERVING	PREPARATION	GRIDDLING TIME	GRIDDLING TEMP
4 people	10 min	12-15 min	375-400°F

Ingredients

- 4 duck breasts
- 1 tsp salt
- 1 tsp black pepper
- 1 tbsp olive oil
- 1 tbsp honey
- 1 tsp thyme, chopped

Directions

1. Preheat the gas griddle to 375-400°F.
2. Season the duck breasts with salt and pepper, then brush them with olive oil.
3. Place the duck breasts on the griddle and cook for 6-8 minutes per side or until they are cooked to your desired doneness.
4. Remove the duck breasts from the griddle and let them rest for a few minutes.
5. Brush the duck breasts with honey and sprinkle them with thyme.
6. Serve the duck breasts hot.

Nutritional Value (Per Serving)

- Fat: 20-25 grams
- Carbohydrates: 2-3 grams
- Fiber: 0 grams
- Sugar: 2-3 grams
- Cholesterol: 80-100 mg
- Saturated Fat: 6-8 grams

SLOW COOKED RABBIT

The rabbit is cooked in a red wine sauce with herbs and onions to give a tender and savory dish that is perfect with a side of mashed potatoes or rice.

SERVING
4 people

PREPARATION
15 min

GRIDDLING TIME
6-8 hrs

GRIDDLING TEMP
275-300°F

Ingredients

4 rabbit legs
1 onion, chopped
3 cloves of garlic, minced
2 cups chicken broth
1 cup red wine
2 tbsp olive oil
1 tsp thyme, chopped
1 tsp rosemary, chopped
Salt and pepper, to taste

Directions

1. Preheat the gas griddle to 275-300°F.
2. Heat the olive oil in a pan, and sauté the onion, garlic, thyme, and rosemary until the onion is translucent.
3. Add the rabbit legs to the pan and sear them on all sides until they are golden brown.
4. Add the chicken broth and red wine to the pan and bring to a simmer.
5. Place the pan on the griddle, cover it with foil and cook for 6-8 hours or until the rabbit legs are tender.
6. Remove the rabbit legs from the pan and let them rest for a few minutes.
7. Serve the rabbit legs with the sauce on top.

Nutritional Value (Per Serving)

Caloric content: 250-300 calories
Protein: 25-30 grams
Fat: 10-12 grams
Carbohydrates: 5-7 grams
Fiber: 1-2 grams
Sugar: 2-3 grams
Cholesterol: 75-100 mg

WHISKEY GRILLED ELK STEAKS

This recipe takes advantage of the rich and flavorful meat of elk, which is marinated in a whiskey, soy sauce, and herb marinade.

SERVING
4 people

PREPARATION
15 min

GRIDDLING TIME
12-15 min

GRIDDLING TEMP
425-450°F

Ingredients

4 elk steaks
1/4 cup whiskey
1/4 cup soy sauce
1/4 cup olive oil
2 cloves of garlic, minced
1 tsp thyme, chopped
1 tsp black pepper
Salt, to taste

Directions

1. In a large bowl, mix together the whiskey, soy sauce, olive oil, garlic, thyme, black pepper, and salt.
2. Add the elk steaks to the bowl and marinate for at least 30 minutes or up to 2 hours.
3. Preheat the gas griddle to 425-450°F.
4. Remove the elk steaks from the marinade and discard the remaining marinade.
5. Place the elk steaks on the griddle and cook for 6-8 minutes per side or until they are cooked to your desired doneness.
6. Remove the elk steaks from the griddle and let them rest for a few minutes.
7. Serve the elk steaks hot.

Nutritional Value (Per Serving)

Caloric content: 250-300 calories
Protein: 25-30 grams
Fat: 10-15 grams
Carbohydrates: 2-3 grams
Fiber: 0-1 gram
Sugar: 1-2 grams
Cholesterol: 75-100 mg

Chapter 10

SEAFOOD RECIPES

GRIDDLED SALMON

The salmon is marinated in an olive oil, garlic, thyme, and black pepper mixture and the result is a dish that is both savory and flavorful, rich in omega-3 fatty acids and a great source of protein.

SERVING
4 people

PREPARATION
15 min

GRIDDLING TIME
8-10 min

GRIDDLING TEMP
425–450°F

Ingredients

4 salmon fillets
1/4 cup olive oil
2 cloves of garlic, minced
1 tsp thyme, chopped
1 tsp black pepper
Salt, to taste

Directions

1. In a small bowl, mix together the olive oil, garlic, thyme, black pepper, and salt.
2. Brush the salmon fillets with the mixture on both sides.
3. Preheat the gas griddle to 425-450°F.
4. Place the salmon fillets on the griddle and cook for 4-5 minutes per side or until they are cooked to your desired doneness.
5. Remove the salmon fillets from the griddle and let them rest for a few minutes.
6. Serve the salmon fillets hot.

Nutritional Value (Per Serving)

Caloric content: 150-200 calories
Protein: 20-25 grams
Fat: 10-15 grams
Carbohydrates: 0-1 grams
Fiber: 0 grams
Sugar: 0 grams
Cholesterol: 50-75 mg

LEMON GARLIC GRIDDLED SHRIMP

The rich and flavorful shrimp is marinated in an olive oil, garlic, lemon, thyme, and black pepper mixture that makes for a beautiful meal.

SERVING
4 people

PREPARATION
15 min

GRIDDLING TIME
8-10 min

GRIDDLING TEMP
425-450°F

Ingredients

1 lb large shrimp, peeled and deveined
1/4 cup olive oil
2 cloves of garlic, minced
1 lemon, zested and juiced
1 tsp thyme, chopped
1 tsp black pepper
Salt, to taste

Directions

1. In a small bowl, mix together the olive oil, garlic, lemon zest, lemon juice, thyme, black pepper, and salt.
2. Add the shrimp to the mixture and toss to coat evenly.
3. Preheat the gas griddle to 425-450°F.
4. Place the shrimp on the griddle and cook for 2-3 minutes per side or until they are pink and cooked through.
5. Remove the shrimp from the griddle and let them rest for a few minutes.
6. Serve the shrimp hot.

Nutritional Value (Per Serving)

Caloric content: 150-200 calories
Protein: 20-25 grams
Fat: 10-15 grams
Carbohydrates: 1-2 grams
Fiber: 0 grams
Sugar: 1 gram

SPICY GRIDDLED SHRIMP

The shrimp is marinated in spicy olive oil, hot sauce, paprika, cumin, garlic powder, and black pepper mixture to make a savory and spicy dish.

SERVING
4 people

PREPARATION
15 min

GRIDDLING TIME
8-10 min

GRIDDLING TEMP
425-450°F

Ingredients

1 lb large shrimp, peeled and deveined
1/4 cup olive oil
1 tbsp hot sauce
1 tsp paprika
1 tsp cumin
1 tsp garlic powder
1/2 tsp black pepper
Salt, to taste

Directions

1. In a small bowl, mix together the olive oil, hot sauce, paprika, cumin, garlic powder, black pepper, and salt.
2. Add the shrimp to the mixture and toss to coat evenly.
3. Preheat the gas griddle to 425-450°F.
4. Place the shrimp on the griddle and cook for 2-3 minutes per side or until they are pink and cooked through.
5. Remove the shrimp from the griddle and let them rest for a few minutes.
6. Serve the shrimp hot.

Nutritional Value (Per Serving)

Caloric content: 150-200 calories
Protein: 20-25 grams
Fat: 10-15 grams
Carbohydrates: 1-2 grams
Fiber: 0 grams
Sugar: 0 grams

GRIDDLED SHRIMP TACOS

The texture of the shrimp and taco is a combination that is unparalleled. The spice kick to this recipe simply makes this a dish that you ought to try.

SERVING 4 people

PREPARATION 15 min

GRIDDLING TIME 8-10 min

GRIDDLING TEMP 425-450°F

Ingredients

1 lb large shrimp, peeled and deveined
1/4 cup olive oil
1 tbsp chili powder
1 tsp cumin
1 tsp garlic powder
1/2 tsp black pepper
Salt, to taste
8-12 corn tortillas
Toppings of your choice, such as diced tomatoes, shredded lettuce, diced onions, cilantro, lime wedges, shredded cheese, and sour cream.

Nutritional Value (Per Serving)

Caloric content: 350-450 calories
Protein: 20-25 grams
Fat: 25-30 grams
Carbohydrates: 25-30 grams
Fiber: 2-3 grams
Sugar: 2-3 grams
Cholesterol: 150-200 mg
Saturated Fat: 3-4 grams

Directions

1. In a small bowl, mix together the olive oil, chili powder, cumin, garlic powder, black pepper, and salt.
2. Add the shrimp to the mixture and toss to coat evenly.
3. Preheat the gas griddle to 425-450°F.
4. Place the shrimp on the griddle and cook for 2-3 minutes per side or until they are pink and cooked through.
5. Remove the shrimp from the griddle and let them rest for a few minutes.
6. Warm the tortillas on the griddle for a few seconds on each side.
7. Assemble the tacos by placing the shrimp on the tortillas and topping them with your choice of toppings.

GRIDDLED SHRIMP FRIED RICE

If you love a bit of rice and you love your shrimp, you've got to try tossing them on with the griddle hay. The soy sauce, sesame oil, ginger, and black pepper add to the smokiness of the barbecue for a great meal.

SERVING
4 people

PREPARATION
15 min

GRIDDLING TIME
8-10 min

GRIDDLING TEMP
425-450°F

Ingredients

1 lb large shrimp, peeled and deveined
1/4 cup vegetable oil
1 tbsp soy sauce
1 tsp sesame oil
1 tsp grated ginger
1/2 tsp black pepper
Salt, to taste
2 cups cooked white rice
1/2 cup frozen peas
1/2 cup diced carrots
1/2 cup diced onions
2 cloves of garlic, minced
2 eggs, lightly beaten
3 green onions, thinly sliced

Nutritional Value (Per Serving)

Caloric content: 400-500 calories
Protein: 20-25 grams
Fat: 25-30 grams
Carbohydrates: 40-50 grams
Fiber: 2-3 grams
Sugar: 2-3 grams
Cholesterol: 150-200 mg
Saturated Fat: 3-4 grams

Directions

1. In a small bowl, mix together the vegetable oil, soy sauce, sesame oil, ginger, black pepper, and salt.
2. Add the shrimp to the mixture and toss to coat evenly.
3. Preheat the gas griddle to 425-450°F.
4. Place the shrimp on the griddle and cook for 2-3 minutes per side or until they are pink and cooked through.
5. Remove the shrimp from the griddle and let them rest for a few minutes.
6. In the same griddle, heat 1 tablespoon of oil and sauté the garlic and onions for about 1 minute.
7. Add the peas and carrots and sauté for another minute.
8. Push the vegetables to the side of the griddle and pour the beaten eggs in the center, scramble the eggs and then mix them with the vegetables.
9. Add the cooked rice and shrimp to the griddle and stir-fry everything together for 2-3 minutes.
10. Stir in the green onions and cook for another minute and serve.

GRIDDLED SEAFOOD PLATTER

This recipe is for those who love the sea on their plate. If you are into fishing, you've got to have this one in your arsenal.

SERVING 4 people

PREPARATION 20 min

GRIDDLING TIME 8-10 min

GRIDDLING TEMP 425-450°F

Ingredients

1 lb large shrimp, peeled and deveined
1 lb scallops
1 lb squid, cleaned and cut into rings
1/4 cup olive oil
1 tbsp lemon juice
1 tsp dried oregano
1 tsp garlic powder
1/2 tsp black pepper
Salt, to taste
Lemon wedges, for serving

Nutritional Value (Per Serving)

Caloric content: 300-350 calories
Protein: 25-30 grams
Fat: 15-20 grams
Carbohydrates: 5-10 grams
Fiber: 1-2 grams
Cholesterol: 150-200 mg

Directions

1. In a small bowl, mix together the olive oil, lemon juice, oregano, garlic powder, black pepper, and salt.
2. Add the shrimp, scallops, and squid to the mixture and toss to coat evenly.
3. Preheat the gas griddle to 425-450°F.
4. Place the seafood on the griddle and cook for 2-3 minutes per side or until they are pink and cooked through.
5. Remove the seafood from the griddle and let them rest for a few minutes.
6. Serve the seafood platter hot with lemon wedges.

Chapter 11

DESSERT RECIPES

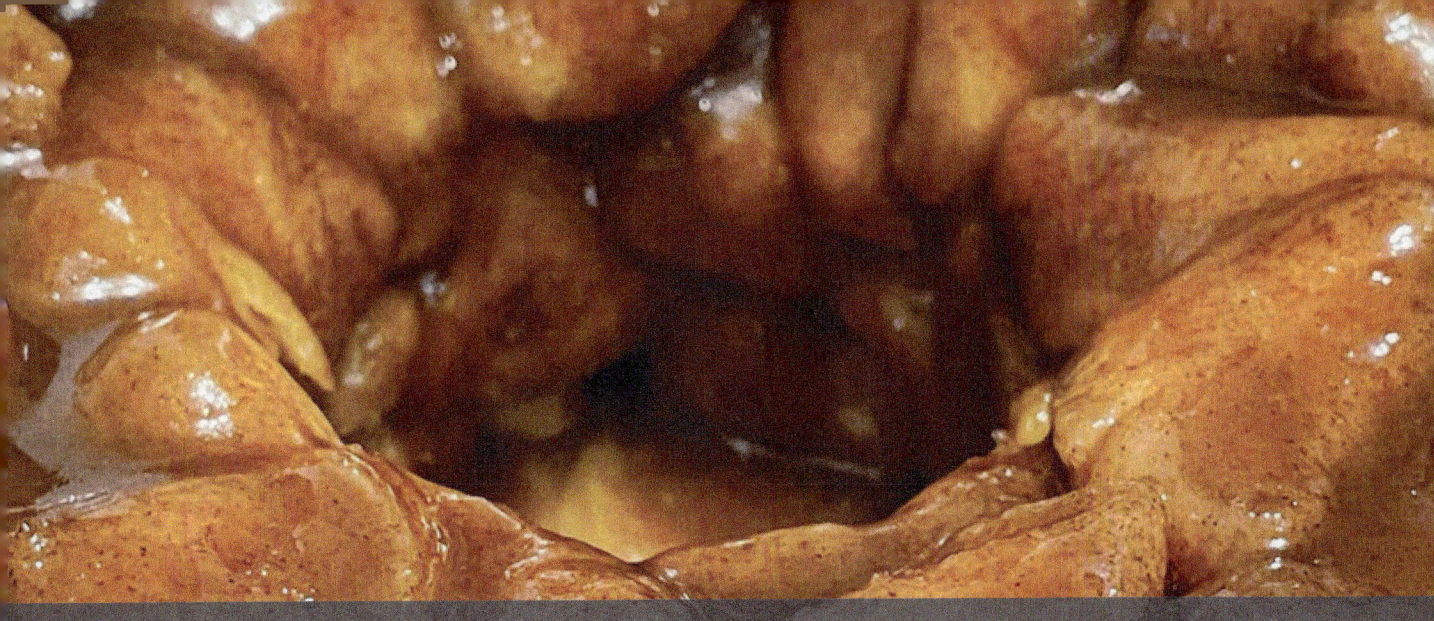

GRIDDLE MONKEY BREAD WITH BISCUITS

Desserts are what separates a master griddle chef from the layman. The dish is both sweet and flavorful, with a nice crunchy texture, and makes for a perfect way to enjoy a comforting treat with family and friends.

SERVING	PREPARATION	GRIDDLING TIME	GRIDDLING TEMP
6-8 people	20 min	8-10 min	375-400°F

Ingredients

1 can of refrigerated biscuits
1/2 cup granulated sugar
1 tsp ground cinnamon
1/4 cup butter, melted
1/4 cup brown sugar
1/4 cup chopped pecans

Directions

1. Cut the biscuits into quarters and place them in a large bowl.
2. In a small bowl, mix together the granulated sugar and cinnamon.
3. Add the sugar mixture to the biscuits and toss until the biscuits are evenly coated.
4. In another small bowl, mix together the melted butter, brown sugar, and chopped pecans.
5. Preheat the gas griddle to 375-400°F.
6. Place the biscuit mixture on the griddle and cook for 4-5 minutes per side or until they are golden brown.
7. Remove the biscuits from the griddle and let them rest for a few minutes.
8. Drizzle the butter mixture over the biscuits and toss to coat evenly.
9. Serve the monkey bread hot and enjoy!

Nutritional Value (Per Serving)

Caloric content: 400-500 calories
Protein: 4-5 grams
Fat: 20-25 grams
Carbohydrates: 40-50 grams
Sugar: 20-25 grams
Fiber: 1-2 grams

GRILLED SMORE'S PIZZA

This recipe takes advantage of the rich and flavorful combination of chocolate, marshmallow, and graham crackers, which are the traditional ingredients in s'mores.

SERVING
8 people

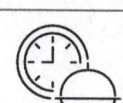

PREPARATION
10 min

GRIDDLING TIME
8-10 min

GRIDDLING TEMP
375-400°F

Ingredients

1 pre-made pizza crust
1 cup chocolate chips
1 cup marshmallow fluff
1/4 cup graham cracker crumbs

Directions

1. Preheat the gas griddle to 375-400°F.
2. Place the pizza crust on the griddle and cook for 2-3 minutes per side or until it is lightly golden brown.
3. Remove the crust from the griddle and let it rest for a few minutes.
4. Spread the chocolate chips and marshmallow fluff over the crust.
5. Sprinkle the graham cracker crumbs on top of the pizza.
6. Place the pizza back on the griddle and cook for another 2-3 minutes or until the chocolate is melted and the marshmallow is golden brown.
7. Remove the pizza from the griddle and let it rest for a few minutes.
8. Cut the pizza into slices and serve warm.

Nutritional Value (Per Serving)

Caloric content: 500-600 calories
Protein: 8-10 grams
Fat: 20-25 grams
Carbohydrates: 60-70 grams
Fiber: 1-2 grams
Sugar: 30-35 grams

GRIDDLE CINNAMON ROLLS

The rolls are sweet and flavorful, with a nice gooey texture and are a delicious and easy-to-make breakfast treat that is perfect for a special occasion or a casual weekend morning.

SERVING 8 people

PREPARATION 20 min

RISING 1 hr

GRIDDLING TIME 8-10 min

GRIDDLING TEMP 375-400°F

Ingredients

1 package active dry yeast
1/4 cup warm water
1/4 cup granulated sugar
1/2 cup milk
1/4 cup butter
1 egg
1 tsp salt
3-4 cups all-purpose flour
1/2 cup brown sugar
1 tsp ground cinnamon
1/4 cup butter, melted
1/4 cup granulated sugar

Nutritional Value (Per Serving)

Caloric content: 400-500 calories
Protein: 5-6 grams
Fat: 20-25 grams
Carbohydrates: 50-60 grams
Fiber: 1-2 grams
Sugar: 20-25 grams

Directions

1. In a small bowl, combine the yeast, warm water, and 1/4 cup of granulated sugar. Let stand for 10 minutes or until the mixture becomes frothy.
2. In a medium saucepan, heat the milk and butter until the butter is melted. Remove from heat and let cool to lukewarm.
3. In a large bowl, beat the egg and salt. Add the yeast mixture and the milk mixture. Stir in the flour, 1 cup at a time, until the dough comes together and is easy to handle.
4. Knead the dough for about 8-10 minutes or until it becomes smooth and elastic.
5. Place the dough in a greased bowl, cover it with a towel, and let it rise in a warm place for about 1 hour or until it has doubled in size.
6. Preheat the gas griddle to 375-400°F.
7. Roll out the dough into a large rectangle.
8. In a small bowl, mix together the brown sugar and cinnamon.
9. Spread the melted butter over the dough, then sprinkle the sugar mixture on top.
10. Roll up the dough tightly and cut into 8-10 slices.
11. Place the cinnamon rolls on the griddle and cook for 4-5 minutes per side or until they are golden brown.
12. Remove the cinnamon rolls from the griddle and let them rest for a few minutes.
13. Serve the cinnamon rolls warm.

EXTRA LOFTY GRIDDLE CAKES

This recipe yields pancakes that are light and fluffy, with a nice balance of sweetness and a crispy exterior. The recipe can be easily modified to suit your preferences, by using different types of flours, sweeteners, or add-ins such as blueberries, chocolate chips, or nuts.

SERVING
8 people

PREPARATION
15 min

GRIDDLING TIME
8-10 min

GRIDDLING TEMP
375-400°F

Ingredients

2 cups all-purpose flour
2 tsp baking powder
1 tsp baking soda
1/4 tsp salt
1/4 cup sugar
1 egg
1 cup milk
1/4 cup melted butter
1 tsp vanilla extract

Directions

1. In a large bowl, whisk together the flour, baking powder, baking soda, salt and sugar.
2. In a separate bowl, beat the egg, then add the milk, melted butter and vanilla extract. Mix well.
3. Add the wet ingredients to the dry ingredients and mix until just combined. Do not over-mix.
4. Preheat the gas griddle to 375-400°F.
5. Use a ladle to pour the batter onto the griddle.
6. Cook the pancakes for 2-3 minutes per side or until they are golden brown and cooked through.
7. Remove the pancakes from the griddle and let them rest for a few minutes.
8. Serve the pancakes warm with butter and syrup.

Nutritional Value (Per Serving)

Caloric content: 400-450 calories
Protein: 8-10 grams
Fat: 20-25 grams
Carbohydrates: 40-50 grams
Fiber: 1-2 grams
Sugar: 10-15 grams

CHOCOLATE GRIDDLE CAKES

If there is one way to make griddle cakes a magical gastronomical experience for chocolate lovers is by adding chocolate to them. And this is how you do it.

SERVING
8 people

PREPARATION
15 min

GRIDDLING TIME
8-10 min

GRIDDLING TEMP
375-400°F

Ingredients

2 cups all-purpose flour
1/2 cup cocoa powder
2 tsp baking powder
1 tsp baking soda
1/4 tsp salt
1/4 cup sugar
1 egg
1 cup milk
1/4 cup melted butter
1 tsp vanilla extract
1/2 cup chocolate chips

Nutritional Value (Per Serving)

Caloric content: 500-550 calories
Protein: 8-10 grams
Fat: 25-30 grams
Carbohydrates: 55-65 grams
Fiber: 2-3 grams
Sugar: 20-25 grams

Directions

1. In a large bowl, whisk together the flour, cocoa powder, baking powder, baking soda, salt, and sugar.
2. In a separate bowl, beat the egg, then add the milk, melted butter, and vanilla extract. Mix well.
3. Add the wet ingredients to the dry ingredients and mix until just combined. Stir in the chocolate chips. Do not over-mix.
4. Preheat the gas griddle to 375-400°F.
5. Use a ladle to pour the batter onto the griddle.
6. Cook the pancakes for 2-3 minutes per side or until they are golden brown and cooked through.
7. Remove the pancakes from the griddle and let them rest for a few minutes.
8. Serve the pancakes warm with butter and syrup.

RUM-GLAZED GRIDDLED PINEAPPLE

Rum-Glazed Griddled Pineapple is a delicious and easy-to-make dessert that yields pineapple that is sweet, juicy, and slightly caramelized, with a nice balance of flavor and a crispy exterior.

SERVING
8 people

PREPARATION
10 min

GRIDDLING TIME
8-10 min

GRIDDLING TEMP
375-400°F

Ingredients

1 fresh pineapple, peeled and cored
1/4 cup dark rum
1/4 cup brown sugar
1/4 cup butter
1 tsp vanilla extract

Directions

1. Cut the pineapple into 1-inch thick slices.
2. In a small saucepan, combine the rum, brown sugar, butter, and vanilla extract. Cook over medium heat, stirring constantly until the sugar and butter have melted and the mixture is smooth.
3. Preheat the gas griddle to 375-400°F.
4. Place the pineapple slices on the griddle and brush the top of the pineapple with the rum glaze.
5. Cook the pineapple for 4-5 minutes per side or until they are golden brown and heated through.
6. Remove the pineapple slices from the griddle and let them rest for a few minutes.
7. Serve the pineapple warm.

Nutritional Value (Per Serving)

Caloric content: 200-250 calories
Protein: 1-2 grams
Fat: 10-12 grams
Carbohydrates: 25-30 grams
Fiber: 2-3 grams
Sugar: 20-25 grams

Conclusion

With this extensive collection of delicious and easy-to-follow recipes, you'll be able to impress your family and friends with your culinary skills in no time. From breakfast to dinner, and everything in between, this cookbook has something for every taste and occasion.

I hope I was able to encourage you to experiment and get creative with this gastronomical art form. The recipes provided are not only delicious but also serve as a starting point for you to put your spin on them. Feel free to swap out ingredients, add your twist, and make the recipes your own. Cooking should be fun and this cookbook is designed to make it just that.

So, there is nothing more to say here; it's time to fire up that gas griddle and get creating. Let's pick up our spatulas and get to work.

CAN I ASK YOU A FAVOR?

Thank you for reading this book, we hope you enjoyed it, and most of all we hope you found it useful!! Please leave an honest review to support Phil's work and the future books he is going to publish.

Reviews help us keep up with your needs and they also help others like you make confident decisions about the best cookbook.

Review or not, we'll still love you!

Best wishes!

Index

CHAPTER 1: BREAKFAST RECIPES	18
Perfect Scrambled Eggs	19
Buttermilk Pancakes	20
Strawberry, Banana, and Hazelnut-Chocolate Crepes	21
Steak and Mushroom Crepes	22
Griddled Cheese Breakfast Burrito	23
Chorizo Breakfast Tacos	24

CHAPTER 2: BRURGER'S RECIPES	25
Juicy Texas Burgers	26
Porky Burger	27
Texas Burger with Beer Cheese Sauce	28
Homemade Veggie Burger	29
St. Louis Gerber Pork Burger	30
White Cheddar Turkey Smash Burger with Apple Slaw	31

CHAPTER 3: VEGETABLES & SIDE DISHES	32
Bacon and Corn Griddle Cakes	33
Hibachi Vegetables	34
Griddle Vegetable Quesadillas	35
Maple Bacon Brussels Sprouts	36
Crispy Fried Green Tomatoes	37
Griddled Vegetables with Melting Aubergines	38

CHAPTER 4: BEEF RECIPES	39
Flash-Marinated Skirt Steak	40
Homemade Meatballs	41
Copycat Texas Roadhouse Steak	42
Griddle Steak Bites	43
Grilled Beef Tenderloin with Herb-Garlic-Pepper Coating	44
Sirloin Wrapped Jalapeño Poppers	45

CHAPTER 5: PORK RECIPES	46
Perfect Pork Chops	47
Smoky Grilled Pork Chops	48
Marinated Pork Skewers	49
Griddled Pork And Peaches	50
Griddle Pork Fried Rice	51
Simple Smoked Pulled Pork Butt	52

CHAPTER 6: CHICKEN RECIPES	53
Seared Chicken Breasts	54
Chicken Teriyaki	55
Chicken Fried Rice	56
Perfect Chicken Wings	57
Chicken Lo Mein	58
Chicken With Mushroom Gravy	59

CHAPTER 7: POULTRY RECIPES	60
Herb Roasted Turkey	61
Marinated Smoked Turkey Breast	62
Brined Grilled Turkey With Maple Bourbon Glaze	63

CHAPTER 8: LAMB RECIPES	64
Griddled Lamb With Spiced New Potatoes	65
Garlic Butter Lamb Chops	66
Garlic & Rosemary Grilled Lamb Chops	67

CHAPTER 9: WILD GAME RECIPES	68
Sweet Jalapeno Grilled Duck	69
Grilled Venison Steak With Balsamic Morel Sauce	70
Bacon Wrapped Venison	71
Roasted Duck Breast	72
Slow Cooked Rabbit	73
Whiskey Grilled Elk Steaks	74

CHAPTER 10: SEAFOOD RECIPES	75
Griddled Salmon	76
Lemon Garlic Griddled Shrimp	77
Spicy Griddled Shrimp	78
Griddled Shrimp Tacos	79
Griddled Shrimp Fried Rice	80
Griddled Seafood Platter	81

CHAPTER 11: DESSERT RECIPES	82
Griddle Monkey Bread With Biscuits	83
Grilled Smore's Pizza	84
Griddle Cinnamon Rolls	85
Extra Lofty Griddle Cakes	86
Chocolate Griddle Cakes	87
Rum-Glazed Griddled Pineapple	88

Printed in Great Britain
by Amazon